"Through Kathryn's deeply personal experience, filled with many powerful lessons, Befriend Yourself will help you feel stronger, happier, and overall kinder to yourself. The practical applications at the end of each chapter, make practicing mindfulness refreshingly accessible. This book is a valuable resource for anyone who is looking to rediscover self love - and really start to see things they like about themselves - instead of being constantly fixated on what they don't like about themselves."

—Andrew J. Kelley (The Boston Buddha)

Kathryn has written a straightforward yet insightful guide to helping anyone, wherever they are on their path, to come back to themselves. I have known Kathryn for many years and her commitment to guiding others to their peace and joy is a true inspiration. I am so thrilled more people will get the chance to experience Kathryn's energy through this book. Befriend Yourself is a beautiful gift to give to yourself or others you care about.
—Max Ryan

MaxRyan.net NYU, ACIM, Law of Attraction, Spiritual Trainer, Livestreamer

"Weaving philosophy, wisdom and science together with personal story, *Befriend Yourself* is both a gift and an invitation to anyone who feels peace, love and happiness are always out of reach. Kathryn Remati gives you the tools and frameworks to find your path and practical tips to walk it. Take this journey with her and you'll discover that every step brings you closer and closer to the home that is your heart *and* that you've been holding the key to it all along."
—Laura Miolla

CEO, Moxielife Coach Inc. and Smart Divorce Strategy

"Kathryn Remati fearlessly shares the story of her heart's healing journey, and in the process, helps us return to the memory of our own wholeness. She compassionately guides us to hold up the mirror to ourselves, shine a light on the darkest areas of our life, release the blockages that have held us back, and boldly step into our best expression. Kathryn is a kind, vulnerable, honest, and insightful guide – making the journey into our healing a beautiful and safe experience. I felt sacredly held throughout every page of *Befriend Yourself* – a must-read on your path to emotional freedom & personal transformation."

—davidji
Author of *Sacred Powers*

"Kathryn Remati is an exciting new voice in the world of self-care. Thoughtful, original, passionate."

—Greg Behrendt
Author of *He's Just Not That into You*, Guest on Oprah, Comedian, *Sex and the City* Writer, Life & Relationship Coach, Cancer Survivor

BEFRIEND YOURSELF

The Self-Love Path to Peace

Kathryn Remati

BALBOA.PRESS
A DIVISION OF HAY HOUSE

Copyright © 2023 Kathryn Remati.

All rights reserved. No part of this book may be used or reproduced by any means, graphic, electronic, or mechanical, including photocopying, recording, taping or by any information storage retrieval system without the written permission of the author except in the case of brief quotations embodied in critical articles and reviews.

Balboa Press books may be ordered through booksellers or by contacting:

Balboa Press
A Division of Hay House
1663 Liberty Drive
Bloomington, IN 47403
www.balboapress.com
844-682-1282

Because of the dynamic nature of the Internet, any web addresses or links contained in this book may have changed since publication and may no longer be valid. The views expressed in this work are solely those of the author and do not necessarily reflect the views of the publisher, and the publisher hereby disclaims any responsibility for them.

The author of this book does not dispense medical advice or prescribe the use of any technique as a form of treatment for physical, emotional, or medical problems without the advice of a physician, either directly or indirectly. The intent of the author is only to offer information of a general nature to help you in your quest for emotional and spiritual well-being. In the event you use any of the information in this book for yourself, which is your constitutional right, the author and the publisher assume no responsibility for your actions.

Any people depicted in stock imagery provided by Getty Images are models, and such images are being used for illustrative purposes only.
Certain stock imagery © Getty Images.

Cover photo and graphics credit: PriscilaSoares.com

Interior Image Credit: Priscila Soares

Print information available on the last page.

ISBN: 979-8-7652-4365-7 (sc)
ISBN: 979-8-7652-4367-1 (hc)
ISBN: 979-8-7652-4366-4 (e)

Library of Congress Control Number: 2023912702

Balboa Press rev. date: 07/31/2023

I dedicate this book and thank Elliot, Ruby and Louie for their unconditional love.

CONTENTS

Introduction ix

1	Vicious Cycle 1
2	Meditation 8
3	Self-Hatred 24
4	Judgment 30
5	Affirmations. 37
6	Mission 42
7	Goals 46
8	Abundance 54
9	Unlearning 62
10	Self-Compassion. 67
11	Letting Go 74
12	Hearts Break Open 78
13	Self-Forgiveness 86
14	Gratitude 93
15	Universal Love. 102

About the Author. 111
Acknowledgments 113

INTRODUCTION

All my life I have felt misunderstood. Although this book may offer a glimmer of comprehension of *my* world, while writing it I came to realize that this applies to everyone. *No one* is ever truly understood, because we are being viewed by others through their own perspective of insecurity and hurt.

True independence is a benefit of fully accepting all misunderstandings as a natural part of life. Self-love and believing in yourself will give you freedom from the chains of other people's judgment. With self-love as your ammunition, you can let go of the rope in the tug-of-war of trying to prove your worth to others. My hope is for what follows to be your passport to releasing the need for outer approval. Travel with your best friend—yourself—to a destination full of wonder that is inside your own heart. Come as you are. You are worthy.

This book will build self-compassion, encourage positive habits, increase self awareness, increase empathy, teach strss management, shift your perception from fear to love, shine a light on your path of purpose, and most importantly, contribute to world peace.

Yes, it takes a shift in perspective to become your own best friend. Looking within yourself with the kind of acceptance and patience you would offer a friend in need is something new to most of us. There are many stepping stones of awareness that must be taken on this path to inner peace with our true inner selves. This book will provide a path through the shady jungle of self-hate in order to reach the warm glowing light on the shores of self-love that only your heart can bestow. If it feels as if you have been at war with yourself, now is the time to surrender to the love that waits for you within.

Loving yourself is the healthiest possible thing you could do! Think about it. When you love someone or something, you give them what they need to thrive without question. If they are thirsty, you hydrate; if they are hungry, you give nourishment. If in pain, you try to alleviate their suffering. You don't wait until the situation is beyond repair to react, whether to a person, a plant, an animal, or even an inanimate object, like a car that needs fuel and servicing.

Giving and receiving love is essential to healing and growth. Applying that love to yourself is vital for health and happiness. So again, please believe me when I say that loving yourself is the healthiest possible thing you could do because of the better choices you will make in every area of your life. It can also be the hardest thing to achieve. Our society is bombarding us with messages of needing to work harder, be better, be this or be that and always selling us something we supposedly need to be deemed acceptable. Commercialism creates and feeds into a sense of lack. The hurdle you must overcome is the lack of belief that you are worthy and deserving of this loving care.

I teach behavioral-modification classes—to treat insomnia, weight, and stress—for a major medical organization. These issues share a common theme at the core that needs to be addressed for positive transformation to occur. That core theme is a lack of self-compassion.

The basic thoughts and beliefs about our own worthiness that reside deep in the subconscious mind influence our emotions, which in turn have an effect on our behavior, resulting in a state of imbalance mentally and physically. With more self-love, we are open to a higher level of joy and freedom from suffering and more balance in our life.

In this book, we will take practical steps that are given at the end of each chapter. I have included exercises that move you toward seeking love via a path through "all the barriers within yourself that you have built against it," to quote the thirteenth-century-poet Rumi. Together, we will discover how loving ourselves can be the vital missing step in achieving unlimited health and happiness. You will learn how to choose to be happy with yourself just as you are. Let me help you see that love is everywhere, and uncover the love that already exists within you and is waiting to shine from deep in your own tender heart.

Pure unconditional love is what you need and what the world needs—right now. Join me as we fill our cup of self-love until it overflows, and we have something truly valuable and authentic to share with the world. We must have the ME love first to be able to spread it out to the world for WE love. You must achieve inner peace in order to spread it around. This is why I have incorporated so much information about meditation. Meditation is for me the path to peace. When you are at peace, you are truly able to give and receive love unconditionally. This of course does not mean that we are without healthy boundaries. It just means we are open hearted to ourselves so we can recognize it in others. It takes a personal revolution to create a peaceful yet effective transformation on a global scale. The aim is to know that one human family of love and acceptance is possible. Achieving planetary oneness through your lens of wholeness.

Self-love is a lifelong process. As we travel on this rickety train, no one can say when we will arrive at our destination, one that offers a profound glimmer of truth, love, and light. But I can tell you that there will be breathtaking views and awe-inspiring stops along the way. If you are ready to take this ride toward magnificent sunsets and beauty within your glorious, messy self, read on as we share this journey along the tracks toward inner peace and love.

VICIOUS CYCLE

Pain is inevitable. Suffering is optional.
—BUDDHA

You may have unwittingly built a fence around your heart that was useful for your survival through a lifetime of painful circumstances. Now that you have decided to do something about it, you need firstly to recognize the symptoms that keep you trapped in a vicious cycle of self-loathing. Getting off the self-loathing treadmill is up to you and your commitment to learning more about your neglected best friend—your sweet self. It is my intention to point you to exit routes that will require your deeper awareness.

The lack of self-love affects every area of our life. There are four main parts that we can begin to work on in order to refill our reservoir of natural love. Let's begin to unravel the blanket of denial to reveal threads of truth hiding in the daily fabric of our thoughts and behavior.

Cycle of Self Loathing

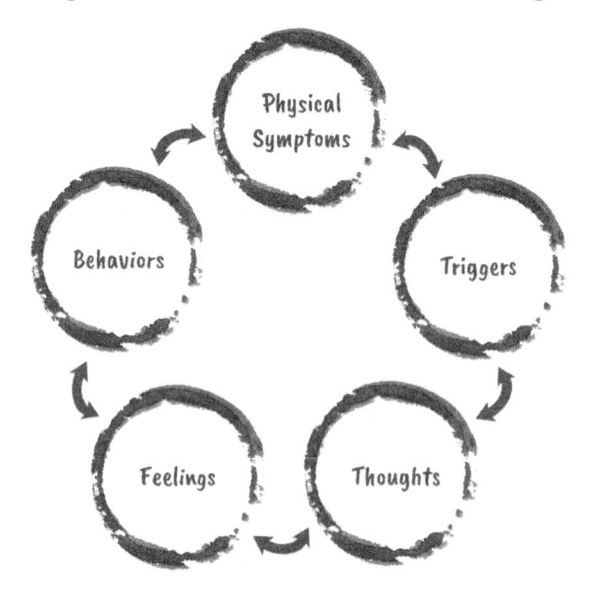

Physical Symptoms → Triggers → Thoughts → Feelings → Behaviors → (Physical Symptoms)

The arrows go both ways because each phase affects the other, and here lies the hope we seek, because each also offers an escape route.

TRIGGERS

Everyone has their own personal triggers to contend with. Most self-loathing can be triggered by any stressful work and/or family situation. Sometimes it takes great pressure while other times our pain is just below the surface. The cycle of self-loathing is interconnected to the various ways we allow our subconscious to sabotage our life. We can be grateful for these triggers, as they alert us to where we need to bring awareness and self-love.

For example, a competitive friend or work colleague may want to prove they are right about something, even something trivial, and this could trigger you into a defensive position. Self-confidence comes from secure knowing that it's OK to be wrong and to be open to learning new things from everyone we meet and from all experiences and behaviors.

Our escape from this is to adapt one of the famous "four agreements" as shared by Don Miguel Ruiz. The wisdom from indigenous Toltec culture states, "Do not take anything personally," which is the second agreement and is a path to self-love that heals our relationship with ourselves and others. What an incredible relief it is to not take anything personally!

THOUGHTS

It is time to bring awareness to the thoughts you are thinking. Are they negative, untrue, and extreme, or even thoughts of catastrophe? These can lead you down a dark rabbit hole to the worst-case scenario. This is not helpful to anyone, ever, except as part of a dramatic movie script. When we activate the inner, judgmental saboteur with our critical thoughts about ourselves and all the ways we are failing or are not worthy in some way, our happiness is stripped from us. Do not believe everything you think, because you can be your own worst enemy.

The escape is to catch yourself and replace critical thoughts with a friendly inner voice by using affirmations and meditation to separate the truth that you are fine in the present moment from the dark stories that pop up from who knows where. All that matters is to bring it out into the light of kind awareness so you can rewire your mind by recognizing the patterns of thoughts that plague you. This will open up some space for peace and self-love that sets your mind free.

EMOTIONS

Our negative thoughts will lead to negative emotions that most of us would rather avoid or repress. Stop labeling them as good and bad or you will find another reason to hate on yourself. Your thoughts are not *bad* and do not lead to *bad* emotions, but they do lead to some kind of emotional response, and it is your task to figure out what your usual responses are. They will rise and fall and come and go. Temporary in nature, just like our thoughts.

Start a healthy relationship with your emotions by learning to accept all of your emotions and view them as temporary houseguests, like in the famous Rumi poem. This is the key to escaping this spiral. Open the door and do not try to rudely push emotions away with overeating, overdrinking, or other numbing tactics. Ignoring them will not get rid of them, so let them in; sit with them awhile until it is time to move on. Don't give them the master suite with the hot tub or they overstay their welcome, and do not throw a sleeping bag on the floor of the basement. Treat all emotions with kind awareness.

Emotions that manifest as anger, sadness, fear, and self-disgust will lead to feelings of unworthiness if not brought out into the loving light of awareness and seen for what they are. They are a passing form of energy in motion. Do not let them turn you into a self-pitying victim. Our role as helpless prey to outside forces will sabotage our happiness and lead to unhealthy behaviors.

BEHAVIORS

How you act upon these feelings when you feel at fault or like you are not enough is the next chain in this cycle. It can cause us to behave in harmful ways. There are, of course, varying levels of self-harm ranging from emotionally eating something unhealthy to isolating ourselves to, at the extreme, overdosing on drugs. Think about the ways you sabotage the most precious prize of your physical health when caught in this ring of revulsion.

The escape from this part of the loop is not simple if you are living with a serious addiction, and in that case, you must seek professional medical help. Most can try to add a healthy behavior to our routine that will turn into a habit that requires no willpower. Exercise that is fun to do—like any team sport, yoga, tennis, golf, or dancing to name a few—will activate the release of endorphins and get us back on the sunny side of the street. Learn to self soothe, otherwise the loop leads to your body reacting adversely to the self-hatred.

PHYSICAL SYMPTOMS

These will occur in response to the unhealthy behaviors you exhibit. Symptoms can be excessive weight gain or loss, skin conditions, and illness in all forms from toxicity to your liver and other organs of the body. When we get to the stage where we become so overwhelmed and distracted by mounting medical issues, we sabotage our health, happiness, and any chance of reaching our goals. To become entrenched in a cycle of stressful self-loathing creates dis-*ease* in our body, mind, and spirit. Self-loathing is a major contributor to stress that eats away at your vibrancy. You may be very judgmental about your body and complain that it is not good enough even though most of it is working correctly trying to keep homeostasis. When you focus on what's wrong with your body, adding hateful thoughts against yourself, you reenter the loop.

The escape plan is simple and can begin right now—we replace any of these stages with healthy and positive options that are discussed in the chapters of this book.

THE SELF-LOVE TEST

Admitting that your present situation is out of balance is the only place to begin your self-love journey. Honesty is the best policy, according to psychologist Carl Rogers, who said, "When I accept myself, then I can change."

Identifying where you are right now will increase your chances of success with your new way of seeing yourself and the world around you, and of loving yourself. Self-awareness is the key to uncovering the truth of who you really are, and that truth is you are a being of love.

If you don't already have a pad of paper or a notebook to write in, I suggest finding something to take notes and use in the future to chart your progress as you learn to uncover internal barriers to self-love that may not be immediately obvious. Together let's look for some clues.

This is a list of signals that represent a lack of love for yourself. Let's check if you may be suffering from some of them:

1. Constantly comparing yourself to others
2. Avoiding looking at photographs of yourself and feeling bad when you do look

3. Being overly opinionated and judgmental, including harshly judging yourself
4. Including something you don't like about yourself during conversations
5. Taking things personally too often
6. Spending too much time with competitive, negative, critical family and so-called "friends" who may in fact be "frenemies"
7. Denying your family had troubles or dysfunction
8. Consistently having an excuse for not reaching personal goals
9. Feeling wrong or guilty when doing recreational activities just for fun
10. Standing in front of a mirror or on a scale as a trigger for anxiety
11. Indulging in extreme consumerism and shopaholic tendencies for a temporary feel-good fix and then feeling guilty about spending money on yourself
12. Being indecisive and making fear-based decisions
13. Suffering from chronic, compulsive complaining
14. Thinking there is something wrong with you that needs to be fixed
15. Micromanaging and finding yourself unable to relinquish control
16. Seeing the worst possible scenario about any situation
17. Accepting the blame even when it's not your fault
18. Avoiding being alone, and when alone, always being distracted with tv, phone, or internet
19. Lacking a hobby or a regular creative outlet
20. Being afraid to make a mistake or admit to having made one
21. Having unhealthy habits such as nicotine, alcohol, or overeating
22. Having workaholic tendencies to avoid self-reflection
23. Spiritual bypassing by not admitting to any type of suffering
24. Using the word *should* a few times a day
25. Being prone to emotional eating
26. Being codependent and perhaps a victim of abuse, abandonment, or alcoholism
27. Feeling a strong need for others to approve of and like you
28. Feeling the need to prove you are good enough
29. Realizing you are addicted to social media

30. Settling for relationships that need you rather than fully love you
31. Being a people-pleaser and excessively nice to the extent that you are unable to set boundaries and say no in an assertive way
32. Suffering from persistent procrastination
33. Lacking trust in your own decisions and opinions
34. Exhibiting extreme perfectionist behavior or having perfectionist tendencies
35. Feeling victimized all the time; taking on the role of victim
36. Needing to be right at any cost
37. Being attracted to emotionally unavailable relationships
38. Realizing that your inner dialogue about yourself sometimes has a harsh, judgmental tone and works as an inner critic that picks on everything, including how you think and behave

If you felt a tinge of truth in any of the above telltale signs of a lack of self-acceptance and unconditional self-love, you now know what behaviors you would like to address. I also suggest taking this opportunity to add a few of your own unique issues to work on. Bring your awareness to what is no longer serving you for your highest good. Your first step is to see what is not working in order to transform it.

Remember to check back throughout the year to see if this checklist has changed for you after implementing the behavioral modifications suggested in the chapters of this book.

PRACTICE

Try sourcing other self-examining tests such as the positive intelligence assessment (PQ) test on the Positive Intelligence website or explore enneagram types.

Journal prompt: Write down five good things others have said about you. How would your friends describe you? Do you believe them? How does this list make you feel?

2

MEDITATION

Quiet the mind and the soul will speak.
—BUDDHA

When I was twelve, my new stepfather moved us to the other side of the world to live in Sydney, Australia. By the time I was sixteen, I was severely depressed, feeling lost and displaced, with a history of traumatic experiences. I was unhappy in a home where no one ever asked if I had homework or took an interest in my future.

My group of school friends were skipping classes to get high and go to the beach. School was like a prison I wanted to escape from. The blaring bell of my boredom rang out as an hourly reminder of how much I hated being there. Obviously, I was failing, and my future was dim. I found myself on the probation list, just days away from being kicked out of high school.

Then, dragging out the trash one spring night, I took a few minutes to sit on the curb that was still warm from the day's rays. Tilting my head back, I absorbed the moonlight and paid homage to the spectacle of stars that danced across the skies of the southern hemisphere. Stars were one constant in a life of confusion and chaos, no matter how often my stepfather moved us or abused us. I wished I were one of those stars. I even had personal names for my favorite twinkling row of distant glows. Somehow, being out there with my star pals, the sadness would surrender just long enough for me to feel safe to be myself—whoever that was. I had no idea, but at least nature helped me feel a part of this world.

As I stood up to go back inside, a piece of newspaper flew onto my ankle from the pile on the neighbor's curb. Standing under a streetlight, I could just make out the words "Mind Development Introductory Lecture." I felt compelled to attend.

The course originated from British educator Alexander Everett. Having been hailed as the father of the Human Potential Movement, Everett founded an elite school in Britain, and was an enthusiastic student of philosophy and theosophy.

After self-healing from polio with the power of prayer and affirmations that he'd learned from the Unity Church in England, he followed his passion to America where he worked with José Silva and began to study techniques of mind control, self-hypnosis, and meditation. With divine intentions, he used some of the Silva techniques in the Mind Dynamics course, as well as concepts from Edgar Cayce (1877–1945). Jess Stearn wrote *The Power of Alpha Thinking* (1969) about Everett and this very program.

The next weekend I was the youngest person sitting in a chair with twenty-five other curious participants who, like me, were not sure what they wanted from this. I began to discover all the marvels our minds were capable of. I learned to go within and use my imagination and intuition for practical solutions in everyday life. My first spiritual experience was not directly from Everett but from an Australian psychologist that adapted and updated the course. He was my first unlikely guru in a suit.

As soon as he entered the room, the entire place felt different. His blue eyes bore into our souls. Throughout the course, I experienced prophetic dreams, astral travel, and energetic shifts all over my body, as well as an incredible physical healing of myself and, remotely, others.

The entire course centered on meditation. All in all, I spent fifty hours, mostly with my eyes closed while learning mind games and secular meditation techniques. Definitely not a cult, this course combined Eastern traditions with the latest brain- and mind-development research. For me, meditation has been and will always be a magnificent life changer.

The weekend made me see myself in a totally new light. I was able to feel palpable peace flow through all the cells of my body, feel the real vibration of love flooding out of my pores, and feel motivated to become one with my true self: the inner self that is untouched by insults, other's beliefs, or negativity from my surroundings.

I was learning to love myself. I thought I was flawed, but came to understand that I was actually worthy of love even though I had no reference or experience yet. It still took decades of what some would call massive failures—but what I would call enormous learning curves—in relationships for me to know myself and to feel deserving of that love inside. This is the recipe I am sharing with you in this book. It's a heavenly cocktail combining meditation with self-love that is good for what ails you.

Learning to meditate turned my life around. It may have even saved my life. I became obsessed with my health. I found new friends to jog with at dawn on the beach before school started. I became a vegetarian and taught myself yoga from one of the many books I devoured daily. My grades went through the roof as I enjoyed studying for tests and going to class for the first time.

I was accepted to university where I was able to quench my thirst for more information on the mind and the brain. I graduated with a BA in psychology. No wonder I am so passionate about meditation. It turned my life around from being a depressed, near-delinquent dropout to achieving at higher education with my future looking bright.

That was in the late 1970s when meditation was a ripple in a lake. By now it has become a fast-moving wave, gaining speed and turning the tide into a major movement around the globe. Meditation is increasingly mainstream, no longer on the fringe like when I taught my friends in my dorm room at college. If someone had told me back then that the world would be listening to my guided meditations on their hand-held phones, it would have seemed like a science fiction fantasy.

These days, we have secular spaces where we can meditate in a group with various teachers. Music and film stars blog about it, and it is no longer exclusively associated with Eastern religion, orange robes, or incense-burning hippies. Anyone can sit on their couch and enjoy a meditation session. Celebrities and doctors are part of the growing list of Westerners spreading the word. Peace is the word and meditation is the way to get it. Time to get on board the meditation peace train.

The discovery of the negative effects of stress on our systems has led to the gradual acceptance in the medical community of the benefits of meditation for relief.

Stress has also become identified as the leading cause of inflammation and disease in the body. Accumulated stress is being blamed for many modern ailments such as heart disease, hypertension, depression, and eating disorders to name a few.

The convincing link between the mind and body is now well established, and health and wellness advocates in the medical profession promote reducing stress to avoid disease. Scientific research continues to add overwhelming evidence on the stress-relieving advantages of meditation. The many benefits to the actual physical brain are being documented, proving that meditation is not a hippie-woo-woo fad but rather an essential part of a healthy lifestyle. Soon it will be more accepted as a wellness essential, as habitual as exercising, eating natural foods, and brushing our teeth.

The build-up of stress in our bodies leads to sickness, tension, and fatigue. Our emotions can become strained and our minds filled with fear and negative thoughts. According to mental health research, intense feelings of anxiety can even cause a nervous breakdown. The nerves don't actually break, of course, but it's a signal to shut down and reset. We have become out of balance.

To reset, begin by closing your eyes and limiting any sensory input. This will immediately start to slow things down. Deep breaths will activate the parasympathetic system that sends a message basically telling us that it's "OK to relax" and that the time has come to switch off the fight-or-flight response, which has become a dangerous default mode of operation for so many. Dangerous due to its chronic nature and the flood of toxic hormones like adrenaline and cortisol that cause wear and tear on all systems of the body, causing inflammation.

A meditative practice has an anti-inflammatory effect on your body. All you need to do to shut down the stress mode is to move your focus to your breath, lowering your brain wave frequency to alpha, the most powerful brain wave.

Simply put, the brain is like a broadcasting and receiving transmitter running on electricity. Like a radio station, it operates on different channels where one predominates at a time. Alpha waves were the first to be discovered by scientists due to their slower, more powerful signal. If you were hooked up to an EEG machine while meditating, it would register an alpha/theta reading depending on the depth of your meditation practice.

The reset button isn't just needed for excess. Balance also needs to be reset due to a lack of something in our lives too. Meditation can fill a spiritual void where there is a lack of purpose, meaning, peace, and love. When we move our awareness from the physical body, calm our emotions, and still our thoughts, what remains? The answer to that question has found both ancient philosophers and new age gurus searching for words to label something there are no words for. You just have to try it for yourself.

Who teaches you to go within and meditate, what the lineage or the mantras are, what part of the world it comes from—that doesn't matter as much as finding a technique that resonates and works for you. There are many meditation paths to inner peace, but they all lead to the same blissful place. Finding the one that fits your lifestyle is as important to your health as daily physical exercise. The mind and body are interconnected, so remember to apply the reset button to balance your inner work with your physical workout.

Sitting in silence can be difficult, though. We have an average of around eighty thousand thoughts per day, and most of these are repetitive ruminations on the past mistakes we think we made and compulsive thoughts of future fears. Silence can become a battle with what the Buddhists call the "monkey mind" as your thoughts jump from one branch of thought to another branch to another, interrupting the flow of peace.

We can't experience peace when we are regretting the past or worrying about the future. This is why meditation is the single most effective tool in our self-love toolbox. It makes us aware of the constant negative way we speak to ourselves. The inner critic is a loud and very often foul-mouthed judge. We would never say these things out loud and especially not to someone we loved. So why do we beat ourselves up like this day in, day out?

Sitting in silence will allow you to be a witness to the parade of thoughts, realizing eventually that you are not your thoughts. They are just thoughts—and a thought can be changed. It no longer controls your life. The Buddha advises to "Rule your mind, lest it rule you." Meditation is a discipline that gives you the opportunity to detach and observe without judgment. You can discover for yourself how badly you need your own compassion, and then start to think more kindly toward yourself.

It may be comforting to know that even the Dalai Lama has thoughts pop up when meditating. The difference is that he just lets it go. You can too, and say "next" when a thought threatens to drift you downstream to a past or future episode. Simply saying "next" and going back to an awareness of what your breath is doing can be incredibly effective. Focusing on your breath without changing or trying to control it is a fitness workout for your brain. Cultivating mindfulness in this way will increase your focus and clarity, which is sadly being shortened daily with the digital speed of a click, shortening the span and depth of our awareness.

Mantras, breath awareness, and guided imagery are all used for meditation, partly to give the monkey mind something to do to distract it long enough for us to find some peace. Mantra is Sanskrit for "mind vehicle," as it is a way for taming and training the mind. Get yourself some mala beads (which are like a rosary but with double the number of beads at 108). Your task is to repeat out loud or silently to yourself a word or phrase 108 times as you slip the beads through your fingers each time to keep track. It takes approximately eight minutes.

Sanskrit is an ancient language and is most useful for its mystical process of making a soulful connection to your inner self. In more logical, practical terms, it offers a sound that the monkey mind finds more difficult to attach a memory or association to. In this way, saying for example, Sri Ram (which just translates to "I am") is a perfect tool to get centered and find that sweet spot of silence, or at least less noise and mental chatter. I have my own favorite chants such as Om Namah Shivaya or a mantra for aligning your vibration with the vibration of abundance: Om Shreem Maha Lakshmiyai Namah.

Another great way to start meditating is with a guided meditation. Guided meditation and visualization is just focusing on a mental picture. This is like focusing on a mantra or on the breath. The benefits are many, and even the most experienced meditator will benefit from a little guidance that can lead gently to that peaceful place in an efficient manner. Anything that takes the focus away from anxious thoughts about the future or replaying past mistakes is a great gadget for goodness.

We do as we are told by the voice, and before we know it, no more body, no more thoughts, just peace. Peeling away the layers until there is nothing but the inner self doesn't have to be a struggle or a chore. Just like exercising our bodies in a fun way with a sport we love, meditating can be fun too.

Whether with longer guided meditations for full-body-scanning relaxation that is an indulgent treat or shorter pick-me-up versions, we can look forward to putting on the headphones to tune out the stress and tune in to our happy place anytime. It doesn't matter if we are sleep-deprived and happen to drift off during the session, because the subconscious mind never sleeps. You can still benefit from the affirmations.

Positive affirmations at a deep level while meditating or sleeping are the best way to rid yourself of repetitive, negative thought patterns. The positive and healing words in a good guided meditation will feed your soul in a way you can't do by yourself without monkey mind waking up. Being gently guided is perfect for anyone convinced that they can't meditate and is also my personal favorite. A gentle voice to lead you to peace can even be helpful with a simple breath meditation.

The addition of meditation into a daily routine can make a huge difference to your overall quality of life, as can practicing mindfulness.

It is difficult to pick up a magazine or scroll through social media without seeing a mention of either mindfulness or meditation. Sometimes it can be confusing, as the terms seem to be interchangeable. Here is a simple explanation on the ways that they are both separate and similar and can synchronize together.

We can start by dispelling two common myths: Mindfulness is *not* thinking really hard about something, which sounds stressful. Meditation is *not* about shutting down the mind like an off switch, which sounds boring and is impossible.

They are something far different—tools to access inner peace, which is already inside of you. They rely on your ability to focus entirely on the present moment. Both offer a way to decrease suffering and increase your level of happiness.

Mindfulness, by definition, is the informal practice of present-moment awareness that can be applied to any waking situation. It is a way of being aware. As Jon Kabat-Zinn states in *Full Catastrophe Living*, "When unawareness dominates the mind, all our decisions and actions are affected."

How often have you driven somewhere only to wonder how you got there because your mind was on autopilot while you were checking into the past or the future, both of which you have no control over? Most of the things you do are done without full awareness.

We eat our meal without tasting it fully; our bodies get wet in the shower while our minds are elsewhere. How many sunsets and smiles have we missed because we felt compelled to check our phones? Our obsession with multitasking is an example of trying to do too much at once without focusing fully on each stage of the experience. Lack of awareness also prevents us from listening to our bodies when they need nutrition, rest, exercise, or hydration.

Mindfulness eliminates stress from a situation by being aware and engaged in the activity while keeping a perspective free of judgment. We aren't trying to guess the future or create a mountain out of a molehill. By getting out of our own controlling way and observing mindfully just what is, without labeling it or placing an opinion on it, we can be free of the stress of expectation and fully accept the moment and all it offers.

Living mindfully means we experience something with what the Buddhists call "beginner's mind." That means we are listening to someone with our full attention on their words, voice, and feelings—as if for the first time—without second guessing, judging, or waiting for a pause in the conversation for our turn to talk. According to the Buddhist monk Thich Nhat Hanh in their book *True Love*, "Listening is an art we must cultivate."

He teaches deep, compassionate listening as a mindfulness practice for enlightenment and to ease pain and suffering.

Obviously, mindful listening improves relationships, because listening with patience, trust, an open mind, and acceptance is going to be a good thing. Coupling that with more conscious control over our emotions can only be monumental for our own personal growth and relationships.

Responding to stress instead of reacting habitually is what Kabat-Zinn calls the "mindfulness-mediated stress response." The usual arguments don't trigger us in the same knee-jerk way. When our buttons are pushed, our reaction time is slower due to a thoughtful presence in the present. When we are aware of someone else's suffering and deeper needs, we don't take things personally. Life becomes less superficial and more compassionate.

Combining the informal, wakeful awareness of daily mindfulness with a formal meditation practice is the most effective way to eliminate stress from our lives. Each enhances the effectiveness of the other.

Closing the eyes and becoming aware of the inner world of your thoughts, bodily sensations, sounds, and energy, while reciting a silent mantra, is using mindfulness as a formal mind-training technique. We need mindfulness to be able to relax and prepare for meditation, for example, when scanning our physical body by focusing on each part. One becomes a component of the other.

Meditation, which I have gone over above, is the more formal practice of minimizing outside distractions to go within by relaxing the body and calming the emotions and thoughts. Awareness of peace is achieved when the parade of thoughts is slowed down and a gap between thoughts becomes clear.

While meditating, we are being mindful of our thoughts from the viewpoint of an observer, without clinging to them. Our thoughts can just float by like clouds while we learn something about our inner selves. We can see how negative our thinking can be or how much time we waste dwelling on the past. This is crucial information for anyone wanting to increase happiness.

You become a witness of the surprising or predictable type of thoughts that flow through you, without chasing them and diving into the story.

Meditating twice a day for ten minutes will reap benefits in your outer mindful life. It is the perfect way to let go of accumulated stress, and results in many health benefits, such as a good night's sleep, more compassionate and peaceful relationships, strengthened brain function, and increased physical vitality. Even your immune system is strengthened from the daily moments of deep restful wakefulness that meditation offers.

It won't take long before you can extend the ten minutes and carry that bliss into your life more and more.

Mindfulness and meditation go hand in hand in creating a happy life, no matter what terminology we want to use.

Pain management is not often discussed alongside the topic of meditation and self-love, yet chronic pain can block both. Meditation can help.

How can you find peace or love a body that penalizes you daily with constant pain? How can you love yourself while experiencing constant hurt? Chronic pain is a part of daily life for millions of people. Experiencing severe to low levels of pain for three months or more is a condition that affects every aspect of a person's life. Sufferers are to be congratulated for getting out of bed to face another day that is continually interrupted by the pain they must endure. It can cost them their overall health, relationships, and jobs.

Whereas an occasional headache or sore muscle pain can be easily remedied with a pill and a good night's sleep, chronic pain is more subjective and more complicated to treat. It has been reported that after similar surgeries, individuals experience different thresholds of pain tolerance as well as the length of time pain is felt. This is where research gets interesting, as it points to the involvement of personality, general health issues, and daily stress levels.

Stress and pain are allies, and how people handle stress and pain is crucial. The two states are intertwined. Pain creates stress and stress adds to the pain. Stress has physical ramifications: it produces cortisol, amyloid plaque, and inflammatory cytokines. If stress is lessened, the pain cycle can be broken.

It is for this reason that holistic and natural approaches like meditation and mindfulness are suggested as part of the overall pain management plan.

There is a Chinese proverb that applies here: "Tension is who you think you should be. Relaxation is who you are." Relaxation is our natural state, and the body is a self-correcting organism that you can assist through heightening relaxation. Meditation activates the parasympathetic system, allowing us to relax.

Meditation has proven to be a pain reliever. It has been studied in patients with fibromyalgia, cancer, hypertension, and psoriasis. Meditation produces a neural chemical change in the brain that normalizes hormones, blood pressure, and airflow, and releases endorphins, serotonin, and dopamine.

Mindfulness has been found to lead to a decrease in pain-related drug utilization, while activity levels and feelings of self-esteem increase, uninfluenced by gender or type of pain.

Guided meditation is the easiest option for sufferers to try because the words and instructions, combined with soothing background music, will move our focus away from the pain to flow toward the peace we long for.

Here are two powerful practices that combine mindfulness and meditation and can be enjoyed in a comfortable position, such as a reclining chair or a bed:

FULL-BODY-SCAN MEDITATION

This calms the physical, emotional, and mental body by returning us to our natural state of deep relaxation. Begin by moving your awareness mindfully over the main muscles of the body from head to foot, releasing stress and letting go completely while giving each muscle total awareness and focus.

To gain mindfulness of the pain, it can help to give it space, a color, a shape, and a texture in order to truly discover what exactly you are dealing with. Ignoring or resisting can create more tension and pain and suffering. Then become aware of where the pain begins and where it ends. Investigate the edges of pain and you will discover the parts next to it that are pain-free. A thorough body scan is the key to starting to unlock hidden emotional and physical tension that can hide in the muscles, causing physical pain. Once the body is relaxed, focus on calming the emotions with positive affirmations such as "I am peaceful," "I am grateful," "I am safe." You can now begin to feel real peace flow through all the cells of your being.

BREATH MEDITATION

This is a classic way to instantly change the way you feel by becoming aware of your breathing. We take over twenty thousand breaths a day, uninterrupted. Breathing is always there in the background. When you take the time to stop and focus on something that is always happening, for just a few minutes, you become grounded in the present moment. Why is this a good idea? Because you can't ruminate over the past or feel anxious about the future when you are fully in the present noticing nothing but your breathing. Stress and the pain it creates is immediately lessened.

Start by focusing on where you are most in touch with the breath as it enters your body. The nose, chest, or belly are where we feel the breath the most. Thoughts will pop up, but you will train yourself to watch them as they float away without your attaching to any of the stories. Letting go of dramas and finding clarity in the here and the now is a healing exercise for pain sufferers.

Meditation and mindfulness are the keys to liberation from suffering, no matter what the actual cause. Simply by implementing a self-care regime that includes some form of meditation, it is possible to feel more peace, happiness, and gratitude for every day

Remember that—just like when trying anything new—commitment, consistency, and compassion are what make our experience a successful one. Start once a day, then morning and night. Like a rusty tap, you may find it is only dripping at first, but in time you will be able to flow in and out of your inner sanctuary with ease and longer lasting benefits.

In the movie *Anchorman 2: The Legend Continues*, which is set in the 1970s, the main character, Ron Burgundy, takes up the new fad of jogging. His friends think he is crazy. While younger viewers might find that reaction absurd, there really was a time when the sight of someone running past you would make you ask, "Where's the fire?" Decades later, jogging is so widely accepted as exercise that if you asked people to name a common means of exercising, running would be one of the first to come to mind.

There are obvious parallels with meditation. But it won't truly become mainstream until more yoga studios and gyms include meditation instruction on their schedules. Additionally, there are numerous practical considerations to holding a regular meditation class in the same location where we exercise our bodies.

Just as science has confirmed the health benefits of jogging, recent research into meditation suggests its benefits may make it something of a fitness regimen for the brain. Over three thousand scientific studies point to too many benefits to list here. The following, however, would be more than enticing to any yoga student seeking health and longevity: increased vitality, lowered blood pressure, higher levels of the anti-aging enzyme telomerase, growth in the thickness of the pre-frontal cortex, increased immunity, lowered heart rate, stronger neural connections, better sleep, and greater relaxation and happiness.

Meditation is an essential self-love tool and can be the ultimate stress reliever, a life skill available at any time of day. As LA-based yogi-monk Steve Ross says, "The peace from daily meditation flows into the rest of your day and transforms your life." Think of meditation as "flexing" the brain so that, like a muscle, it grows stronger with use.

Yoga studios and gyms are perfectly positioned as one-stop locations for the health conscious to care for the inside as easily as the outside. Meditation is for everyone—even the type-A gym junkie. And keeping everything in one location minimizes the driving, parking, and preparation. Making meditation more accessible to everyone often means holding classes in a neutral location, without connection to particular beliefs. Many people are not comfortable entering a Zen center or ashram for meditation instruction.

Also, it is simply not true that meditation demands a perfectly quiet environment. Alan Watts, Western philosopher and author of *The Way of Zen*, put it this way: "If you can't meditate in a boiler room, you can't meditate." Of course, beginners might need a slightly more conducive environment, and a yoga studio or fitness center can be the perfect place for them to explore meditation within a class of other curious seekers.

All yoga classes can give clients an element of inner peace, but they may need additional stress relief at times. After all, stress can start to build again right after class—as soon as the phone starts ringing, while running late for an appointment, while you are trying to find the car keys in the bottom of your gym bag. Not to mention our to-do lists, which only get longer as the day progresses.

No one can escape stress no matter how much you work out, and even the most fit and flexible among us may suffer from stress-related disorders such as anxiety, insomnia, fatigue, headaches, and skin conditions.

You may want to try a guided meditation class. Once clients have begun to experience those effects, their lives become more relaxed. They will be calmer in situations that used to trigger stress, and will return to class for more. Gyms and studios will likely find that adding a meditation class to their schedules creates a new area of healthy activity, and their participating clients will have gained a priceless stress-management tool in their wellness toolkit.

The truth is that many people have only a vague idea of what constitutes meditation, believing the myth that it necessitates shutting down the mind or that it just means concentrating really hard on something. They may also see it as a religious practice, paying money to take a nap, or just a boring waste of time. Many also simply believe they cannot do it.

It is the job of the health practitioner to educate the fitness-conscious public on the benefits of meditating. Part of the service a practitioner provides should be to help clients understand the latest research supporting the practice of meditation. Too many advertise a holistic wellness approach but without offering meditation classes.

Encouraging gyms or yoga studios to offer meditation classes as healthy lifestyle options can be as easy as chatting with the owner about your interest in building your brain as well as your muscles. Maybe suggest a move-and-meditate class that begins with a shorter series of poses followed by a brief meditation.

When approaching a studio, remind the owner that yoga goes hand in hand with meditation. The Vedic etymology of the word "yoga" is "to join" or "to unite," and we believe that to be the union of mind, body, and spirit. Also adding a meditation class would facilitate a complete yogic experience. The goal is to create not just a leaner, healthier physique but a happier whole person, inside and out.

Socializing has been redefined by our technological lives and has never been so easy, yet maybe it's too easy and making us a little too comfortable with our solitude.

We spend a lot of time alone without realizing it. It may not seem like you're alone when you're on Twitter, sharing images on Instagram and Pinterest, and liking friends' updates on Facebook, but nonetheless scrolling is a solitary pastime. It keeps us in one place and time flies by. No wonder it seems so difficult to add fifteen minutes of meditation into a daily schedule.

Nothing can compare to an in-person connection. Being face to face, with genuine 3D laughter and sharing ideas, feels far better than reading a text and misunderstanding the intended meaning of the typed message because it didn't include a smiley face emoji. Go for a real smile on a real face more often.

You may want to consider joining a group of like-minded souls for meditation, even if it is just once a week. Get rid of the restricting idea that you can only find inner peace when you are alone. Sure, meditating alone at home is great, but like listening to music at a public performance, group meditation has some unique benefits.

Here are five excellent reasons to meditate with others:

1. Everything is better when shared, including meditation.

Feel a real connection by tapping into the same silence and source of peace at the same time. Steve Ross, who taught Russell Simmons and Dr. Oz how to meditate, says that "the fundamental reason why group meditation works well, especially for beginners, is that the group dynamic uplifts and empowers everyone present. This doesn't require belief, just observation and experience."

2. Meditating with a group helps to develop a habit.

At home, it is too easy to find excuses to walk past that meditation cushion for another day. Going to the gym is routine for many of us, so finding a meditation group to help us form another good habit makes sense. By doing so, the health of both the mind and the body can be checked off our to-do list.

3. Feedback is available.

Meditation groups often include practitioners at varying levels. If new to meditation, you may find that other members of the group can help clear up confusion over different types of meditation or can address possible difficulties with the practice. They may also provide feedback regarding experiences that arise during the meditation process.

4. Joining a group is actually physically good for us.

Loneliness is now proven to be bad for our health. According to *Bowling Alone: The Collapse and Revival of American Community* by Robert D. Putnam, joining a group can cut your risk of dying in the next year by half! An environment of acceptance and belonging are perfect conditions under which social animals like us can thrive.

5. Be a part of the bigger picture.

A group can better support an individual's inward journey. It is inspiring and motivating to connect with others who might share our greater good intentions for world peace. It is easier to apply Gandhi's suggestion to "be the change you wish to see in the world" when you are part of a collective crowd. According to Andrew Kelley at The Boston Buddha, a common group goal can "collectively unify and add strength to our intentions," even if the goal is just to be more relaxed and less reactive.

PRACTICE

The gap between thoughts widens with practice and they start to still. Every day is different, and even after decades of daily meditation, I can honestly say no two sessions are the same. Why should they be? We are not the same person as yesterday.

Try a meditation for yourself by choosing one of the above methods, or join a class online or pick a track from the *Tranquil Me* meditation app.

3

SELF-HATRED

If we could see the miracle of a single flower clearly, our whole life would change.
—BUDDHA

You know that ghost: the phantom with all our secrets and shame that hides in the shadows buried deep beneath our outer identity. We cover up our deep-rooted insecurities, terrified and waiting for the day when we will be revealed as impostors unworthy of love and happiness. We wear a mask to hide the broken, incomplete, less-than-perfect human we are certain that we are.

Suppressing our shame is exhausting. Forcing on new masks to keep up with constantly changing circumstances creates stress on an existential level; striving to have the outer trappings of success in order to fool the world into assuming we are not lacking. The cracks start to show when our eyes and mind focus on a mirror and find that, after all our efforts, we still only see the deficiencies, the not good enough, reflecting back to us. The chasm between inner and outer realities cripples us with the illusion of lack. We are unable to shape our own destiny because we focus on who we are not. Our lack of self-worth influences every decision we make, whether about relationships, career, or health.

The part of us we loathe is sometimes referred to as the shadow self, embodying our traumatic, shameful, hurtful, excruciatingly disappointing past experiences; it's the one we keep in the dark, hidden and dormant, or so we think. Unfortunately, every feeling and memory we try to repress is reflected in an outer reality. We are looking through a filter of fear. Our perception of the world around us has to be affected.

William Blake, the nineteenth century poet, artist, and prophet, was noted for the fine line he walked between genius and insanity. He wrote the following profound words: "If the doors of perception were cleansed everything would appear to man as it is, Infinite. For man has closed himself up, till he sees all things thro' narrow chinks of his cavern."

I know this to be true firsthand, thanks to a weekly therapy session I attended with the purpose of saving my first marriage. The objective was not reached, although I still gained invaluable life lessons.

It had been suggested that I try one-on-one counseling, and at this session, my wise therapist was ready for me. She knew I had something buried, and she was not letting me out until it was out. Like extracting a rotten tooth with her questions, she zeroed in on me and had me squeezing the arms of the chair. Then, gently ensuring that I felt safe, she listened as I spoke of sexual abuse when I was eight years old, something I had never told a soul before that day. I could barely admit to myself that it had really happened.

It did happen. During that session, the emotion came flooding out along with my shame. I no longer had to carry this burden. After I revealed my dark secret to my highly intuitive psychologist, I wondered how she knew. Was she psychic? She didn't need to be—she had a well-trained eye. I had been presenting all the signs of a victim of abuse.

The most amazing thing happened as I walked out of the office after this transformational encounter. Confused, I looked down and ran my hands over my skirt to feel if it was still there and if I had remembered to put on underwear. I was feeling naked and exposed. With relief, I looked around and asked my therapist how the flowers I saw were planted so quickly that day. It turns out that the rows of vibrant multi-colored petals that suddenly overpowered me with their fragrance and beauty had always been there to greet visitors at the entrance to her office, but I'd never seen them until that day.

Bricks of hurt and humiliation that I had constructed around my heart began to crumble, just enough to let in some light of acceptance and for me to come to my senses—literally. As the artist Matisse shared, "There are always flowers for those who wish to see them." Until that day, when I finally let my guard down and the truth out, I'd been unable to see them; I had been living like a little black cloud in a dress, just going through the motions in a haze of memory suppression.

This is but one highly personal example of how your perception and the way you relate to others is dramatically altered by your hidden feelings for yourself. When your consciousness is expanded by love, you see, feel, hear, smell, and taste things differently. Incredibly, your mindset, how you perceive the world, is formed from your level of inner worth. Your perception is what you need to focus on. You have already wasted too much time caring about other people's perceptions of you. In the words of Dr. Wayne Dyer, "Hostile people live in a hostile world and loving people live in a loving world."

Growing up, I was a poster child for self-hatred. Hopefully, my testimony here will be illustrative, an example of a transformation from self-hatred to self-love. My self-hatred stemmed from the constant lies my mother and stepfather fed me about my real father, whom I loved and who profoundly shaped the nature of my future relationships by being the first man I cherished. When I was forced to turn against him and take sides, I started to believe that if he was "garbage," I must be half garbage too, just by sharing his unworthy DNA. I was told he rejected me and if I ever found him, he would hurt me.

This led to underlying abandonment issues that haunted my every decision with self-doubt and a fear of inadequacy. I had been relocated to the other side of the planet, making it nearly impossible for me to contact my father. Remember that as I was embarking on my teens in the late 1970s, snail mail and curly-corded phones were the order of the day. At first, my father's birthday cards were marked return to sender, bound for the US. Plus we moved every two years around the northern suburbs of Sydney, thanks to the con man my mother had married, which made it impossible for my father to find me. As the evidence presented by my mother during my formative preteen years stacked against him and the case for his rejection of me continued, my self-esteem dropped more and more, and the void inside me grew deeper and darker.

It took thirty-three years of separation before I was reunited with my loving father, who turned out to be just the opposite of what I was told.

Then I discovered the chapter about parental alienation syndrome (PAS) in Alec Baldwin's *A Promise to Ourselves*. When I realized that my circumstances had a name and that I was not alone as a PAS sufferer, it felt like a miracle had occurred. PAS had affected my self-esteem at a root level. I had been unconsciously walking through life as if sharp rocks were in my shoes, thinking that this intolerable state had to be endured. I was living proof of the Buddha's number one rule that life is suffering.

Reading Eckhart Tolle's description of the "emotional pain-body" created another crack to let light in. The light that Tolle's words let in flooded my entire being with hope. He describes it as an entity lodged in your mind and body made up of every emotional pain you have ever experienced. It feeds on more pain and drama; but once you become conscious of it, this negative energy field begins to dissipate. It only has strength when you are unconsciously playing out deeply embedded patterns from the past. I had been hooked on the drama, but finally I was aware of it!

This was the first time a label had been given to the monthly production that thundered down on my relationships. My mother had a pain-body the size of Ohio, where I was born. This negative energy was her legacy to me and it hurt. Added to which was all the abuse from my stepdad and siblings, which created a massive pain-body that could lash out like a wounded lion.

That collective hurt lay dormant most of the time until my hormones made it so much easier for it to be triggered. This came to the fore during my second marriage, when I realized I was a PMS control freak psycho-bitch living in denial and worried about another divorce. So I went to work on becoming aware of this emotional monster and killing it with kindness.

Dragging that life-sucking vampire out into the light will turn it to dust, thus allowing the inner light of self-love to break free a little more. Our old wounds are healed by awareness; then we may walk toward the future with the burdens of our past alleviated in order to interrupt the destruction of the present.

What had ailed me had finally become visible. The prognosis was excellent. I absorbed the contents of Tolle's book in order to learn how to dissolve this entity of darkness feeding on my agony. Bringing it into the light with mindful presence had a miraculous effect. To this day, it still occasionally rears its ugly (but much smaller) head—but as soon as I look at it, the awareness shrinks it more. Without turning this into the confessional diary of a reformed drama queen, let me assure you that there is an ocean of peace beneath those turbulent waves.

According to cellular biologist and meta physician Bruce Lipton, as well as other scientists and psychologists, our self-limiting beliefs begin to form at a subconscious level as soon as we can use our ears in the womb up until around the age of seven. Kids are little sponges, soaking up the flood of information released by naïve parents as they battle with their own emotions and mental, physical, and spiritual challenges. Childhoods vary, of course, ranging from the humblest starts in life to the other extreme—prep schools and nannies. None are perfect.

What has become obvious is that a perfect childhood does not exist, and that it is actually our purpose in life to study ourselves, to become more Jedi-like and unlearn what we have learned, in order to grow regardless of the hand we were dealt. To move forward, we need to put together the pieces of acceptance, forgiveness, and empathy from the past. Somewhere along that process, we must connect the most important piece to the puzzle: self-love. It is always there, waiting for us beneath the unconscious patterns.

Many decades ago, Abraham Maslow placed self-actualization at the top of his pyramid as the measure of maturity. His theory is a classification system represented in the shape of a pyramid that illustrates the priority of human needs that are met by an individual growing and transcending through their life stages. Basically, the larger bottom level of the triangle is physiological, then moving up to safety, next is relationships, then esteem and the top is the achievement of one's full potential. Self-love is necessary at every level. These are the reasons we do what we do, but it cannot be done without love of self. Overall, though, these theories are extremely limited in application. Our beginnings are just that: the beginning. The sooner we drop being the victim in our childhood story, the sooner we can connect with our true selves and begin a positive life of peace stemming from self-compassion.

Do not confuse the term self-love with selfishness or narcissism. The aim is to feel the same feelings for yourself as you would toward an innocent, sweet little baby who relies on love to live. Babies survive due to our unconditional love for them—no matter how many diapers we change or sleepless nights we have to suffer. We want and need the same love for our fully grown selves.

We want to take Elizabeth Gilbert's advice to "embrace the glorious mess you are." It is difficult to improve on her phrase, which says it all. It is time to shine the light of love on the ghosts of our past and move forward.

My hope for this book is that it will give you some practical tools that have been invaluable to me in my journey from self-hatred to self-love.

PRACTICE

Choose a day for silence. Plan your own silent mini-retreat where you can commune with nature, engaging all senses, and avoid other people to minimize the risk of speaking. Spend quality time alone without your phone or other distractions. Eat a slow and mindful lunch. Journal any thoughts that pop up. Use it as an exercise in detaching from the mental chatter. Meditate. Reflect and rest.

4.

JUDGMENT

*Do not judge yourself harshly. Without mercy
for ourselves we cannot love the world.*
—BUDDHA

Judgmental thinking and the constant comparison and criticizing of ourselves means that we are also doing this to others. It's time to stop judging your body and everyone else's. Judgment is the crook of connection. It steals our happiness as it closes our hearts. Buddha also said, "Do not be the judge of people, do not make assumptions of others."

World love and human togetherness is our goal.

We have normalized judgmental thinking for ourselves, so it has become the default mode of our existence and is a reality of epidemic proportions. Ask yourself if it is fair to apply this harshness to others who are also doing the best they can under their own circumstances. We must overcome this habitual picking on ourselves so we can stop ourselves before we do it to others. Breaking the chain of judging is necessary to increasing loving.

Breaking this habit is not going to happen easily. We are so conditioned that we use it to make a friend by belittling ourselves. Attend a social gathering and notice the common enemy of hating something about yourself. Any physical or mental attribute will do, any body part. Just mention how much you hate something about yourself and similar sentiments will be echoed back from another self-hater. It is so easy to list all the things we hate about our physical appearance, awful habits, inadequate bank accounts, bad memory, and other perceived flaws. The list is endless. When we stop doing this, we give others permission to give themselves a break too.

We want to love ourselves as we are right now and not wait until we lose weight or have that perfect job or relationship. In fact, all those things will only fall into place after we accept ourselves unconditionally.

Weight is an issue surrounded by judgment, and it keeps us from self-love. Be mindful of your feelings and thoughts around the term "obese" before and after reading this section. There is more to it than meets the eye!

The wellness movement is leading the way for the compassionate movement when it comes to weight. We have opened our minds to new ideas on health, and now the time has come to unlock our hearts for acceptance and unconditional love to flow to all people, no matter their shape or size.

Larger individuals of all ages are much more than a medical term or a BMI classification. It is a normal existence for over 650 million out of the 1.9 billion who are overweight, which is 39 percent of the adult global population, according to the WHO.

Obesity is officially an epidemic, according to recent studies published in the *Journal of the American Medical Association*: "The prevalence of overweight children, adolescents and adults in the United States has increased over several decades." This is not just an American issue though; it is a worldwide development.

A more holistic reference point concerning the overweight in our society is necessary for understanding the whole person, inside and out. It is the first step to a less superficial and more loving world.

Do not confuse compassion with pity. This is a call for better understanding those people who have been misunderstood most of their lives. If you are overweight, or know someone who is, here are a few facts that prove there are instances where the larger individual can be perceived as more than an intentional consumer of calories. They are deserving of love from us and from themselves.

The root causes and triggers that lead to unhealthy weight start far back in our evolution. The human brain has craved high fat and sugary foods since prehistoric times, in order to prepare for a long lean winter in the cave. Our primitive brain still has those cravings, but they are now easier to appease due to the evolution of our culture of convenience. Our ancestors were also more physically active than we are. The scientific community has coined the term "sitting disease" to describe the growing prevalence of a modern tech-obsessed sedentary lifestyle. It seems logical under these circumstances that the population would grow heavier over time.

The subconscious mind is always awake and ready to be influenced by those knowing how to reach it and affect our behavior. Brian Wansink, PhD, director of the Cornell University Food and Brand Lab, researches the "hidden persuaders" used by supermarkets, restaurants, and food marketers. External stimuli such as music, room color, and label design can encourage us to "mindlessly" eat more calories than necessary.

The average American home now has more television sets than people. Research shows a strong correlation between TV viewing and weight no matter what age or what is being watched. Television, YouTube, video games, and the addiction to our phones cumulatively take away time that could be spent for physical activity, distract us from listening to our bodies, and encourage unconscious eating while we scroll or channel surf. We are bombarded with advertising for high-calorie gooey pizza and other so-called comfort foods to soothe our emotions rather than face them.

Research links sexual abuse, early childhood trauma, incest, rape, and molestation with obesity. It has been scientifically proven that more than half of all obese females have had to endure a painful and harrowing event in their past. Psychologically, the weight may help them feel safer and protected from future assaults. Overweight people have not only extra physical weight, but also must deal with more emotional and mental weight than others. We need to end the judgment. Everyone deserves a discrimination-free safe space to exist.

Feeling shamed and singled out by bullies is a common dilemma for the overweight. Our society likes to single out heroes and villains and feed into the drama of winners and losers. Celebrity magazines sell us stories that make anyone that gains weight the "bad" guy. Bullying on all media, social or otherwise, is so prevalent that a new meaning for the word "troll" and "trolling" has had to be added to the dictionary. We are constantly encouraged to compare ourselves with others rather than to see similarities.

Maybe it's because we judge ourselves so harshly that we are less compassionate with others. If we wish to see others in a compassionate light, the best place to begin is to befriend our own worst enemy—ourselves. In the words of Rumi, "Find the sweetness in your own heart, then you may find the sweetness in every heart."

> Find the sweetness in your own heart that you may find the sweetness in every heart.
> - Rumi

This advice from the wise poet may not be as easy as it sounds. Loving yourself unconditionally can be a lifelong process. An essential first step is to improve your self-talk and quiet the inner critic that judges and condemns your actions and feelings. Making friends with yourself begins when we mentally speak with kindness and a gentle, lighthearted tone. Next time you step on the scales or pick apart what you glimpse in the mirror, speak to yourself with kindness and no judgment. Use a term of endearment as you would to a dear friend. What a difference you would make if you replace judging your body with encouragement.

We must all try to love ourselves and others without conditions. Loving what we consider faulty, yet makes us unique, helps us to see the overweight population as lovable too. Let us also accept it as a call for love and treat all beings with compassion.

We can shift our focus from seeing only laziness or gluttony in an individual with a weight problem to an expanded awareness that includes their heart, soul, and suffering. This will go a long way toward building a truly compassionate society. We need to stop shaming, blaming, and separating ourselves from others, and to accept and value all human beings no matter their shape and size.

Next time you face your own judgmental thoughts, replace them with this classic Buddhist meditation of loving-kindness:

> May all beings be happy.
> May all beings be healthy.
> May all beings be peaceful.
> May all beings be safe.
> May all beings be loved.

Everyone wants better health, but without self-love, do they feel deserving of it? Loving yourself is essential because you will make healthier choices to support your miraculous body that you truly love. You will find fun ways to move and lighten up physically, emotionally, and mentally. You will strive for wholeness rather than perfection.

Healthy weight requires a balance between mind, body, and spirit. We must consider the first four letters of the word "healthy" to be reminded that healing is necessary for optimum health. You need to heal and rebalance with natural food, regular movement, a compassionate calm mind, and the spiritual nourishment of self-compassion.

If you eat even after you feel full, then you are eating for the wrong reasons, often seeking fulfillment through food by eating out of boredom, loneliness, anxiousness, or tiredness. Emotional eating is easily triggered by any kind of stress, and we have all been victims of it to varying degrees. Eating for any other reason than the need for nutrition can become habitual when we feed ourselves without awareness, without being mindful and slow. Shop mindfully by listening to your intuition at the store or trying a new type of store to keep your diet flexible as well as interesting. Stock up on an abundant supply of self-love to stay on the healthy path and to feel full and satisfied by an inner sense of security.

Meditation will help you stay focused on healthy weight goals and create more peace and calm in your life to help avoid stress eating. Here are a few affirmations for success with better health:

> I am healthy and happy.
> I nourish my body with fresh food.
> I am open to change.
> I am relaxed and calm.
> I love walking and being active.
> I drink more water to stay hydrated.
> I love my body unconditionally.
> I eat only what I need.
> I find healthy ways to comfort myself.
> I am full of life.
> I enjoy taking good care of myself.
> Change is good for me.
> I see my body as an amazing miracle.
> I feel good about myself.
> I eat only when I am hungry.
> I make healthy choices.
> I radiate health and vitality.
> I am lovable and lighthearted.
> I befriend my body.

PRACTICE

Think about the cultural pressure to be a certain way that leads to judgment. I call it the Barbie and Ken Doll Syndrome.

Write down a list of messages on judgment you have picked up from society. Here are a few examples you can start with if you like:

>A woman must wear makeup to be attractive.
>A man must have six-pack abs.
>Wrinkles are ugly.
>Cellulite is abnormal.
>A tiny waist is attractive.
>You must be married by age thirty.

It is time to release the false beliefs we have been burdened with!

5

AFFIRMATIONS

Whatever words we utter should be chosen with care.
—BUDDHA

Our feelings direct our behaviors, and our feelings are affected by our thoughts. It can all begin with a simple thought, and luckily for us, a thought can be changed. We do not have to allow mean, self-critical thoughts to influence our decisions.

While your internal dialogue can be your own worst enemy, it can also be an opportunity to forge a wonderful friendship with yourself. Speaking to yourself as you would to a best friend or a loved one can begin right now. The way to do this is with affirmations.

The goal is be kind and speak to yourself with patience and the same kind of loving tone you would give to someone you care about and would not like to see suffer unnecessarily. Toward that end, through affirmations, let's create an inner voice that is friendly and supportive; a voice that can pick you up, instead of bringing you down.

First we need to be aware of how many times a day we think we "should have" done better in some way. Every time you "should" on yourself, you are implying that you are not good enough and somehow bad or lacking in some way. Catching yourself whenever you say "should" is a simple thing you can do starting right now.

When you catch yourself saying "I should," just replace it with "I'm doing the best I can." Because that is what is always so true! That may sound like using a cup to catch an overflowing river, but it is an incredibly effective first step in calming that sea of doubt and in turning the tide of negativity.

Because our brains so readily accept the negativity and false facts we feed it, five positive sentences are necessary to combat one negative thought! Luckily, the latest research reveals that you can reprogram your brain thanks to its neuroplasticity. And it turns out that the brain loves firing up new and exciting neural pathways at any age.

Louise Hay is a firm believer in the power of affirmations. In *You Can Heal Your Life*, she recommends repeating positive phrases like a mantra and writing them down. When you put a positive phrase down on paper, she claims that you are casting a spell. That the origin of the word "spelling" comes from the power of writing things down. By giving it your awareness, you are giving it life and invoking a powerful law of the mind.

Thoughts create our reality. By refocusing and redirecting your energy into a positive direction, you are recognizing where you are sending your attention, which will allow you to stop wasting your power on things that aren't supportive of your growth. Recognizing means retooling and resetting your mental machinery. The brain is ready for a reset, so let's get started.

You can begin by placing affirmations on notes around your living and workspace to feed your mind, both consciously and subconsciously, with the kind of loving messages you want to live by and make wonderful decisions by. In turn, this will create the wonder-filled life you desire and deserve. Your positive statements will be soaked up by the brain the same way the ugly, mean statements have been, and with repetition, they will also become a deep truth in time.

Louise Hay suggests that the affirmation "I Approve of Myself" is so powerful that it cannot be repeated or thought too many times in a day. An alternative phrasing is "I Accept Myself Just as I Am."

There is a method to the mystery of affirmations. They resonate at the deeper levels of the brain and mind we need to reach. These levels are easily accessible through meditation, but they must follow certain guidelines. The brain is very literal. You must be careful what you wish for. Use only present tense and positive words.

For example, do *not* say, "I will not be around toxic people." Remove negatives: remember, we are *affirming* not negating! The word "not" in a sentence will have no effect other than to produce the same results. Saying you do not want "toxic people" in your life only reinforces their hold on you. It is like saying "I won't think about a red elephant!" Well, you know what happens next …

So instead, I suggest you turn that sentence into "I only surround myself with positive, supportive people." What a difference that will make!

One key thing about affirmations is that they must be in the present tense to be effective. The brain hears the future tense in "will" and places our desire into a distant tomorrow that never actually comes and is therefore unattainable.

This is why most affirmations begin with the words "I am." Dr. Wayne Dyer offered insight into the spiritual power of those two words. There is great significance associated with the "I am" as acknowledged by many wisdom traditions. Whatever words follow the "I am" will have a powerful effect. "Redefine your self-concept," Dr. Dyer says, "by choosing the words that you opt to place into your imagination. Try this rewording of your inner world as a beginning step to accessing the assistance of your higher self and fulfilling your desires."

There are people who are not comfortable saying affirmations in the present tense because their conscious minds resist too strongly and make them feel like impostors. When they hear "I am living an abundant life with more than enough" or "I love myself unconditionally," it can seem far-fetched, causing their egos to resist the affirmation.

Initially, some of us receive some pushback from the mind when we state certain phrases, such "I am lovable." The mind may respond, "Are you kidding?" Be strong and continue to face that voice with the new positive and truthful statement. You are planting a new belief into an old system, and the new belief begins as a small seed. With repetition and time, it will grow enough to uproot and replace the old belief completely. You will be moving forward.

You can also alter the traditional affirmation with the word "process" and say "I am in the process of loving myself unconditionally," or "I am in the process of bringing balance into my life." This is a wonderful way to get around any blockages or resistance. I must thank my friend and spiritual teacher Max Ryan and his website MaxRyan.net for this concept. He has a wonderful and simple way of making universal laws applicable to even the most skeptical among us.

Words have a vibration. Positive words vibrate with positive energy. Somatic experts have confirmed that saying your affirmations out loud is a powerful technique for connecting the mind with the body. It is a beautiful thing to be in a deep meditative state as you plant these positive seeds into the fertile soil of your open, loving mind.

Yet, you do not need to concentrate or remain focused on them for them to work their magic. Affirmations can play quietly in the background as you do housework, or while you are asleep, exercising, or commuting. They will even work hanging around your walls, mirrors, and doors, from a Post-it note. Your subconscious mind is active and alert at all times of the day or night. It will absorb these affirmations and accept them as truth. The more they are played, the more the neural pathways are reinforced and can reprogram the mind for the loving, positive results you seek.

Here are a few to get you started:

> I am enough.
> I am patient with myself.
> I love myself unconditionally.
> I am lovable.
> I am perfectly imperfect.
> I befriend myself.

PRACTICE

On my *Tranquil Me* app, you can listen to over one hundred self-love affirmations. Pick ones that resonate with you and say them or write them in a journal as many times as possible this week.

6

MISSION

Your purpose in life is to find your purpose.
—BUDDHA

You may be wondering what makes me so qualified to write this book. Why should you take my advice?

Because I am one of you. I know what you are going through. In fact, there was a time when I checked off 90 percent of the self-love test symptoms myself.

I have experienced self-hatred, and I understand how it can sabotage your potential and true calling. I have overcome major amounts of shame, guilt, and negative programming from my childhood using the meditative tools I am sharing with you.

One of my successes in life has come through my voice. If you have allowed me to put you to sleep or listened to any of my other guided meditations then you may not believe this, but I used to *hate* my voice more than anything. I remember painfully listening to my voice on an answering machine and cringing and complaining about the sound of it. Hearing the sound of my own voice had the same effect as a dentist's drill.

At the time, I was a spiritual student, absorbing beautiful inspirational works from every new age, self-help, and metaphysical book I could consume. I was studying psychology and was an avid reader, trying to figure out what was wrong with me. I may have had knowledge, but that didn't make me wise. Wisdom comes from our wounds, and that was the one place I was not looking. Those were buried where I hoped no one would find them, including myself.

I will share with you something that happened to me as a teenager. I was recording my voice into a cassette player as part of an application to a prestigious drama school when my mother came into the room and told me I was vain to record my voice and actors are the most insecure people on the planet and I must be stupid, then left the room. The worse thing for a young teen is to be called "stuck up" or too good for others. It was an insult to tell someone that they loved themselves too much! I immediately switched off the recorder and threw away the handbook, along with my dream of studying at the National Institute of Dramatic Arts. A dream died while another level of self-loathing began that very instant.

It doesn't take much to plant that seed of disgust and disdain for oneself. Especially when you are young—it can be such a simple thing. (When I brought this hurtful encounter up decades later, my mother had no memory of it.)

It took years of self-discovery for me to be in the place I am now. The subconscious mind is extremely powerful, and it cannot be bypassed with knowledge alone. I had to do a lot of work. And now my voice is listened to by thousands of people around the world. I am beholden to the many wonderful reviews that tell me my voice is a gift that brings them peace. It turned out to be my dharma. I am able to contribute to world peace one peaceful person at a time, and now I am able to leave a legacy of love by making this planet a little better through simply using my voice as an instrument of peace.

To be able to do this represents such an incredible testament to how much I have grown in my journey of self-awareness and self-love.

That is why deep in my heart I know that it is possible for anyone to find that sweetness inside by shifting the way they see and speak to themselves.

Who knows what contribution you will be able to make by chiseling away at the self-hatred hiding all that talent and love you have to share. You will uncover a masterpiece just like any great sculpture. Michelangelo believed that every block of stone has a statue inside it and that it is the sculptor's task to find it. He wrote, "I saw the angel in the marble and carved until I set it free."

What will you set free? What talent of yours is hiding under those negative, deeply rooted lies that you still believe about yourself? Are those things that you loathe really true? Of course they are not true, and it's time to plant positive seeds that will result in positive results.

It is so common for us to find out later in life that we have a gift or talent. Maybe you are good with kids and a great teacher, or have a gift for organization or gardening or fashion. Whatever it is, it comes to the surface for many reasons, often due to a change of life circumstances, and it's never too late. There is a way to get the ball of self-discovery rolling a little faster and in the right direction just for you.

Finding your passion and purpose does not have to be a world-shattering contribution that requires venture capital. Let's just remove those kinds of expectations and start right where we are right now. One place to begin is in your own neighborhood, by seeing where there is a need, and by helping to fill that space with love in action. Keep it simple yet effective. There is so much to do in our own community

Imagine how the world would be if everyone helped out in their own corner of the planet. Small steps make big differences. An internship or volunteer work can lead to expanding your zone of comfort to a point where you are placed in an environment that brings out the unique talent that you were unaware that you had.

As taught by Andrew Kelley, The Boston Buddha, in his MFE meditation teacher training, there is a prophetic practice you may also have heard Deepak Chopra use. These three "soul questions" are yours today. In a meditative and relaxed state, ask yourself:

Who am I?
What do I want?
What is my dharma/purpose?

Give yourself as much time as you need to reflect before going to the next question. One at a time, see what pops up. Sometimes you will get an immediate answer and other times it may take days of journaling. It's all good and a worthwhile enterprise.

7

GOALS

One moment can change a day. One day can change a life. One life can change the world.
—BUDDHA

You deserve to change your life with healthy goals. Meditation is a great way to maximize goal achievement. By meditating, you will be able to access the true power of the mind that connects you to the finer dimension of reality. The mind resides in every cell of the body, yet it is not physical. It is a finer substance, an energy that generates *from* the brain. Mysterious and marvelous at the same time, it is your link to self-improvement.

One thing we know for sure is that thoughts emanate from the brain and mind to create our life and lead us to every success or failure. Are we starting each new day with the same old thoughts and expecting different results? When it comes to achieving goals, we are given the advice to "just put our minds to it," yet are never told exactly how we are supposed to do that.

The brain is an amazing electrical and chemical universe, far more complex than any other known living system. It processes up to a hundred million pieces of incoming information from our five senses every second. Its abilities go way beyond the most sophisticated computer, yet at a basic level it is very similar to a computer. We aren't given a user's manual for the brain, but it does come with some automatic programs built in, ones that require no conscious thought, such as our breath, our heartbeat, and our digestion process to name a few.

Later on, we add a few programs of our own, such as negative thinking ("I am not good enough") or caution ("Better safe than sorry"). Perhaps someone tells you "Don't be so stupid" too many times, and before you know it, somewhere in the deep recesses of your mind, the belief that you are stupid takes root. Without awareness, we are all victims of early childhood programming.

These negative beliefs have far-reaching effects on goal completion. We become painfully aware of this when we hit another roadblock to success, whether from procrastination, quitting too soon, or choosing the path of most resistance. These false beliefs about ourselves generate fear of success, and we become self-fulfilling prophecies of failure.

When the control center of the brain is influenced by past negative experiences, fears, and beliefs, you can replace these self-imposed limitations with positive beliefs. You have the amazing ability to instruct yourself to be the loving person you want to be.

Begin a meditation practice and become a witness to your thoughts. Awareness of your own self-talk gives you insight into negative programs that have made their way deep into the mind, becoming a part of the self-limiting belief system that is sabotaging your self-love goals, and any others you have, for a healthy and happy life.

Centering yourself with meditation is like sitting in the eye of the storm and feeling calm, loved, and safe. It takes you to a place where infinite potential resides—at our core, where there are no labels or judgment. Meditation is the avenue to expanded awareness and a shift into a new positive direction.

Meditation sheds light on the negative beliefs that limit us. It is a highly effective tool to access the deeper levels of the mind and reprogram the brain's computer-like mechanisms. You can then let go of old beliefs that no longer serve you, replacing them with new, positive core beliefs that describe your true self. Your true self is already programmed for perfect health and happiness. Your job is to return to that place and clean the mirror of illusion by replacing fear with love.

By going into the deeper level of the mind, you can enhance your sense of self-worth and modify other behaviors. But to be effective, the "instructions" you give must be in a language the brain understands. Since we don't dream in words, visualization is essential. There are three main steps to reprogram for success.

First, set an intention. This could be a physical goal (remember the mind and body are linked): maybe a healthier weight or healthier skin. It could be a mental goal: maybe better grades and stress-free exams or a fulfilling new job. We can also choose an emotional goal: healing a relationship or finding more patience in our daily lives. Consider also choosing spiritual intentions, such as compassion, forgiveness, and service to humanity.

Second, enter a meditative state. Close your eyes to limit outer distractions, take a deep breath to activate the parasympathetic system that shuts off the flight-or-fight mode, and dive in to your well of inner peace. Take your time. Scan the body if you have time and relax any tense areas. Remember this is time just for you, so you can relax physically, calm your emotions, and find your center.

Third, use visualization. The subconscious mind utilizes pictures to communicate with the brain. A picture can paint a proverbial thousand words, and you can use the visual imagination to create the results you want for the highest good. This is easy if you see it all on the big imaginary screen of your mind. Everyone is now so accustomed to staring at their phone, TV, and computer screen, so this is a great place to start for a manifestation-meditation exercise.

Imagine a big white empty canvas, and place it at a distance in front of you, elevated on a stage. Visualize it as large as you want. You can make it simple, with a modern look, or ornate, with curtains or a gilt frame like one of those beautiful art deco cinemas. Make it uniquely yours, memorable; the actual screen is white. Take a few moments to design and build your projection screen.

Next, place yourself in the middle seat of the theater, directly in front of the elevated screen.

Now, visualize a white light around the screen to highlight your positive outcome.

Are you ready to choose a goal you would like to achieve (which we call an intention) and gently bring it to mind?

Yes you are!

You may see yourself achieving physical goals by visualizing a healthier version of yourself on the screen, or see yourself on a vacation or healing a relationship.

Once you have chosen your first goal, sit with that intention and try to focus on the positive outcome you desire. See yourself up on the screen acting as if the goal you have in mind has already been achieved. You are the director, cast, and crew. Be creative and see your personal intention come to reality in your own way as you watch this movie of success.

See what it looks like to have achieved this goal. Where are you? See all the details. What color is the room you are in, or the sky? But don't just see it; try using all your senses and feel it. Touch the fabric of that new dress, the car, the piece of furniture, the leaf in nature, or the sand between your toes.

Taste the healthy food you now choose or the celebratory glass of champagne or the favorite meal cooked in your honor.

What does your scene smell like? Did someone bring you flowers? Or do you smell the fresh ocean air?

Listen to the sounds of your success too. Is there an announcer's voice? Cheering and applause or ocean waves lapping on the shore?

Remember to have fun as you see your image of success in all its details on the screen of the mind. Hold up those grades! Put on that medal! Shake hands with that new boss! See yourself celebrating! Up on the screen, see the reactions of the people in your life. They are happy for you. Make sure to add lots of positive emotion to the scene. It will add energy to the intention. Feel the joy and exhilaration of achievement. Embrace the experience as fully as possible.

Wayne Dyer adds emotions to the manifestation process noting that they add power to the intention. "The universe will begin to conspire with you," he says, "to fulfill your wishes. That is the law of co-creation" (from *Wishes Fulfilled*). Therefore, you must get excited and tell yourself that this is most definitely achievable, and it is a done deal because you have literally put your mind and emotions on it at the most effective level possible.

Try to bring to mind your movie screen anytime you feel a need to reinforce your goal. Always only see the white-light end result, and remember to keep your eyes closed, allowing your images to gently rest and filter into the depths of your inner mind.

The time always comes when we have to leave the movie theater and trust in the visions. All you have to do at that stage is let nature takes its course, making sure to listen to your intuition. Let the brain and mind find the fastest route to the outcome you desire while you remain open to spontaneity and make sure not to override your inner guidance with logical, critical analysis, or by being a control freak.

We know from studies that the brain and body don't discriminate between sensory images in the mind and what we call reality. Our brain filters information according to these goals and images in order to lead us in the direction toward our intended outcomes. These principles of the mind are always at work, but unless we learn, with meditation practice and visualization, how to harness this power through focus at a deeper level, our goals can go the way of most plans: down the drain with excuses. Blaming outside circumstances or berating ourselves only perpetuates the cycle of failure.

You can now use your brain to help you become the person who makes exciting things happen in life. Life is so short and each day so precious. Did you know there are only four thousand weeks in an average human lifetime? The Buddha says, "The trouble is that you think you have time." Drifting through life hoping things will change while you stay the same underutilizes both your brain and your extraordinary potential.

When you believe you are worthy, your life will reflect that worthiness, and you will literally see the good things that were right in front of you all along, including opportunities for success.

It is a wonderful feeling to begin loving yourself, to take time for healing and rest, and to get to know your wounds and shadow side. Yet be careful not to confuse self-indulgence with self-love. I once found myself in that trap and gave myself a little too much permission that got tangled up with things not so good for me, like too much screen time, too much food I liked, and too much time wasted by laziness. I thought I was giving myself a break and spoiling myself, but I was spoiling the present moment with purposeless nonactivity. I lacked a consistent morning routine because I would remember all the years raising children and having to be on call all night and early mornings. I used to dream about the freedom to sleep in late that I now had as an empty nester, but I over did it, especially during COVID lockdown. Self-love became self-indulgence, which can open the door to old patterns.

Self-love affirmations and meditation combine to present a powerful yet passive route to recognizing your worthiness. But they must be backed up by positive action and a healthy dose of discipline. I am still getting over my personal aversion to the word discipline. Maybe if your family was like mine and dished out discipline in a very violent, heavy-handed, and unpredictable way, you didn't like it either. I feared discipline because I equated it with severe punishment. I find it difficult to force myself to do anything on a regular basis because I was raised in a chaotic household. Chaos felt comfortable, since it was all I knew for so long.

Now I understand that discipline is the healing modality I need the most in my life. I need to relax in the routine, knowing I will show up for myself even if no one else is able to provide me with stability. I see how a repetitive daily activity can create gain from my pain. My greatest life lesson is to trust myself to create my own environment of safety. I am the only one that can give myself the peace I desperately need in my life. Discipline will heal and transform your storms into a rainbow of promises to yourself that you keep. That is real self-love. Doing what you said you would do will build a pattern of integrity. I love the following anonymous quote:

> Thoughts become actions,
> Actions become habits,
> Habits become our character,
> Becoming our destiny.

Nothing is more effective at changing your life than love in action. Past trauma is stored in the body and within the subconscious mind. To effectively reprogram deep-seated beliefs from the past, we need to make a physical change of some kind.

Forward motion is easy with a few behavioral-modification tools. Bad habits will not just magically disappear. They must be replaced by healthy ones. Say that you eat for all the wrong reasons. Wouldn't it be great to have healthy eating behaviors, and ones that are automatic too? This takes time and repetition, but it works due to the reticular activating system and creating new neural pathways in your brain.

Healthy options such as mindfully and slowly moving your body by attending all types of yoga classes or trying tai chi will open you up to new experiences and people while you benefit mentally and physically. Learn more about somatic therapy, which connects the body and mind to release past trauma, increase self-awareness, reduce pain, and give you a better night's sleep, to name just a few of the benefits.

Any kind of exercise, whether aerobic, strength, or stretching, will release endorphins and other "happy" hormones, leading you to the exit door of the self-loathing room. Keeping this promise to yourself is like drinking a self-love potion that fills you with faith and builds on itself.

To build a new pattern of success, begin with something small and definitely achievable. For example, decide to increase your daily step count. This is a simple way to start a ripple effect into every avenue of your life. Give yourself every opportunity to achieve your goal. Leave a pair of sneakers in the car to take advantage of an unplanned opportunity for a walk, or park the car farther away from the front door. Taking the stairs instead of the escalator is another option. Keep track by noting the days in your planner and ticking them off.

You can also ask a friend to keep you accountable or join you for a nightly stroll. So many drop off the trail they are creating because they did not want to ask for support. Maybe thinking "I have to be strong and do it on my own" has gotten in your way in the past. Think about it. Why do people volunteer to help others and do charitable acts without compensation? The answer is simple: It feels good! We all *love* to be helpful.

But don't be afraid to ask for help. People are flattered when you ask for their input, and are more than willing to offer their time and energy.

Another option is reaching outside your comfort zone, maybe to someone not in your immediate circle who exhibits a healthy lifestyle. Vulnerability is our greatest strength. Why? Because it gives others permission to expose their own soft little underbellies. Hey, making new friends is always a plus. And don't hesitate to ask a friend of a friend for advice in the right circumstances.

Keeping promises to yourself is the best way to feel better. Building trust builds integrity. You will be showing yourself that you can be trusted; that you are no longer the type of person who is easily fooled. You will now know that when you say something, you mean it. No more excuses that were lies to yourself. When you make these changes, self-approval easily follows.

It is axiomatic that success breeds success. Baby steps grow, and you will find yourself able to handle more and more. Then the day will come when you look around and realize your unlimited potential. Your achievement is real—it is not just a complacent type of optimism when it is grounded in actual daily results.

PRACTICE

Make sure your goal is achievable and specific, and use a method of keeping track of your daily achievement, like a journal or calendar. Success and a pat on the back from your best friend—yourself—will go a long way to building a destiny full of love for your amazing self. Use these affirmations before and after you complete your new healthy habit:

> I say yes to life.
> I trust myself.
> I am confident and courageous.
> I am enthusiastic and decisive.
> I can do anything I set my mind to.
> I am ready for success.

8

ABUNDANCE

Give, even if you only have a little.
—BUDDHA

You deserve an abundant life. This goal of living an abundant and happy life with all your creative and financial needs met is why you work so hard every day. When working harder and longer hours isn't being reflected back to you in your bank balance, we need to look at our mindset about money.

Abundance, or lack of it, is connected to feelings inside of us. These feelings come from our past experiences. According to Eckhart Tolle, "A person's thinking and beliefs are conditioned by their past: their upbringing and culture they live in." Negative experiences as a child can create a scarcity mindset. If we overheard our parents fighting over money, we may relate acquiring affluence with instability and fear. A chaotic family life where there was never enough money, but plenty of drama around the subject, can create deep patterns of resistance such as blaming others for what we lack, overspending to fill a void, or hanging on too tight for fear of running out of it.

We live in a world where the messages of scarcity are all around us. We must buy everything on sale, we must not overspend, we must think what we have is never enough. We are victims of a scarcity consciousness that affects our actions and perceptions.

Many of us are unable to free ourselves from the burden of guilt we feel from ignoring the class structure that confined our parents. Making over a certain amount can cause shame and feelings of unworthiness, leading to the sabotaging of success without being conscious of what is really happening at a deeper level.

Such mindsets can hold our earning potential hostage. If we have a failure mindset, we are fighting the natural flow of the universe, always swimming upstream and wondering why we don't seem to be getting anywhere.

We need a whole new perspective on wealth. Money is just an energetic vibration, like anything else in the universe. Why do we surround it with negativity, believing that money and spirituality, and money and love cannot coexist? Of course they can and they do.

According to Deepak Chopra, abundance and affluence is our natural state, and all we have to do is "restore the memory of what we already know." He says that according to quantum physics, when you give something away, you automatically create a vacuum that will be filled with more of whatever you gave away.

Therefore, the key to attracting more abundance is to give. Give and you shall receive! It's a law of the wisdom traditions, one we need to apply to our lives, whether it is an abundance of love, joy, health, or yes, even money. Notice your resistance to the word "money." This is due to an acquired limited generational belief that clouds your perception. Money is just energy, so quit blocking it with a cringing combative attitude. You deserve money as much as you deserve love. Love, money, and spirituality can coexist in harmony. Going with the flow of abundance includes attracting money with generosity.

Self-love means you are deserving of prosperity in all its forms. You can use the wellness tools of visualization, affirmations, and awareness of self-talk to shift your money mindset from one of lack to one of plenty.

At any time, you can choose the future you want, and begin to make changes for your highest good. Think about it. Our present predicament is a result from a decision and a thought we had in the past. A life of abundance can be as simple as imagining a better future now.

Experience your own guided imagery meditation for a few minutes, twice a day. Using the image of a river flowing with water or anything that represents abundance to you, such as gold or silver, is a start. See yourself swimming in abundance.

A river or ocean is particularly powerful, as the origin of the word "currency" is the Latin *currens*, which means the "condition of flowing," as in the flowing or circulation of money. We must vibrate at the level of what we wish to attract, and money is just a form of energy, like everything else vibrating in the world. The more you practice silent time with your true self, the easier and more effective it becomes, and the more it flows. Before you know it, the flow is full of miracles and more.

Meditation shifts our energy from wanting and struggling to a positive, active energy of purpose, intention, and prosperity. It helps us stop living on automatic, unconsciously going through the motions as dictated by a fearful past, and lets us discover the truth within. It is time to stop blaming society and our past, and to take control by shifting our mindsets from lack to plenty.

Changing your self-talk is another method to unsnarl past programming. Substituting our chosen self-talk, in the form of affirmations, can end the self-defeating negative way we perceive the world. If we have convinced ourselves we aren't good enough, perfect enough, old enough, young enough, smart enough, fast enough, rich enough, or lucky enough, then we need to wise up to those lies. They only produce frustration. We need to start speaking the truth about ourselves. The truth is that we have unlimited potential and power within us. We can get back into harmony by changing our thought patterns and starting to believe in something more honest and empowering. It is time to shift our mindsets from lack to plenty. To quote Glinda the Good Witch, "You had the power all along, my dear."

You can begin by writing down affirmations. Here are some to start with:

> I am smart enough to succeed.
> I am releasing the past and letting it go.
> I am truly lucky and blessed.
> The universe is abundant and there are plenty of great jobs for me to enjoy.
> I choose to see myself as successful and happy.
> I am open to opportunities.

You can then read these affirmations, starting in the morning and as much as you can through the day until right before sleep. Reading an affirmation as the last thing you do before sleep will carry it into your subconscious where the past programming has been stored.

Here is a list of affirmations for abundance:

- I am full of gratitude.
- I am abundant and prosperous.
- I am richly rewarded for my time.
- I am generous.
- There is plenty of everything for everybody.
- I am fulfilled.
- I am showered with possibilities.
- I live a plentiful life.
- I am universally provided for.
- I attract only goodness, love, and positivity.
- I am open to the flow of wealth.
- I vibrate at a frequency of overflowing plenty.
- I am positive and plentiful.
- I attract positive people and events.
- I am showered with all I need.
- I am enough.
- I have all I need inside of me.
- I am peaceful and plentiful.

- There is always more and more.
- Prosperity overflows in my life.
- Money flows to me in abundance.
- My choices lead to abundance and prosperity.
- I am time-affluent.
- Prosperity within me, prosperity around me.
- I am surrounded by choices.
- Abundance within me, abundance around me.
- I allow all good things to come into my life, and I enjoy them.
- I have an abundance of possibilities.
- I naturally attract abundance and prosperity.
- I live with plenty and possibility.
- I am in harmony with the universal flow of abundance.
- Abundance and prosperity are my birthright.
- I am in a state of fulfillment.
- I have an abundance of love and joy in my life.
- I am free to do whatever I wish to do.
- I say yes to life.
- I am prosperous, healthy, and happy, and live in abundance.
- I am thankful for the abundance and prosperity in my life.
- I am a magnet for money.
- Prosperity is drawn to me.
- Money comes to me in expected and unexpected ways.
- I am worthy of more money.
- I am open and receptive to all the wealth life offers me.
- I embrace new avenues of income.
- I welcome an unlimited supply of income and wealth in my life.
- I surround all money with positive energy.
- Money is energy that flows to me.
- I use money to better my life and the lives of others.
- Wealth constantly flows into my life.
- I attract opportunities that create more money.
- I can handle large sums of money with ease.
- I am at peace with having a lot of money.
- I can handle massive success with grace.

- Money expands my life's opportunities and experiences.
- Money creates a positive impact in my life.
- I am worthy of a wealthy life.
- Money comes to me in miraculous ways.
- I am deserving of abundance in my life.
- I am open to receive wealth in many ways.
- I have the luxury of time.
- I love my positive, happy, abundant life.
- The more I give, the more I receive; the more I receive, the more I give.
- There is plenty for everyone.
- I am open and receptive to all the good and abundance in the universe.
- I have unlimited choices; opportunities are everywhere
- I support others in becoming prosperous, and in turn, life supports me in wondrous ways.
- I now do work I love, and I am well paid for it.
- I am now willing to be open to the unlimited prosperity that exists everywhere.
- Money is a state of mind that supports me.
- I allow prosperity to enter my life on a higher level than ever before.
- Life supplies all my needs in great abundance, and I trust life.
- I radiate success, and prosper wherever I go.
- The law of attraction brings only good into my life.
- I move from poverty thinking to prosperity thinking, and my finances reflect this change.
- I enjoy financial security.
- Whatever I appreciate, appreciates.
- Each day brings wonderful new surprises.
- I am worthy and deserving.
- I deserve the best, and I accept the best right now.
- I have an attitude of gratitude.
- I am limitless.
- I am a magnet for success.

- I am unlimited potential.
- I show up for opportunities.
- I say yes to possibilities.
- My energy matches the energy of prosperity.
- I am always in the right place at the right time.
- Money flows to me effortlessly.
- I have a positive money mindset.
- I am well compensated.
- I have financial peace of mind.
- I can achieve anything I set my mind to.
- I share my good fortune.
- I lovingly accept all gifts given to me.
- My life is such a miracle.
- I am a master manifester.
- My thoughts manifest a healthy, wealthy life.
- My deepest desires are easily fulfilled.
- The energy and vibration of prosperity becomes one with my peaceful loving energy.
- I am truly lucky and blessed.
- The universe is abundant and there is plenty for me to enjoy.
- I am generous.
- I choose to see myself as successful and happy.

PRACTICE

Listen to the Abundance meditation on my *Tranquil Me* app and even fall asleep to it playing quietly next to your bed.

Try also using this chant to the Hindu goddess of abundance, Lakshmi, saying it 108 times using your mala beads:

Om Shreem Maha Lakshmiya Namah
Om Shreem Maha Lakshmiya Namah
Om Shreem Maha Lakshmiya Namah

Another great chant is Shreem Brzee, saying it 108 times in the morning and night. It takes me about eight minutes each round. If you are consistent twice a day for a month, you will be so busy with opportunities, you may be forced to stop the chanting for a while!

Meditation and chanting is a way to clear these blockages once and for all. Going within to the unlimited field of possibilities will free you of labels, resistance, judgment, and fear. It will break through the hypnosis of social conditioning surrounding money.

9.

UNLEARNING

Don't believe false doctrines.
Don't follow the way of the world.
—BUDDHA

You may wonder why loving yourself is so difficult; it's probably difficult because the way of the world is negative. We are bombarded by messages from media and culture that the aim is to be perfect when perfection does not exist—not even in nature. Think of a two-headed mushroom: it is perfectly imperfect, yet we still believe in an unachievable ideal for ourselves. Negativity that feeds into your internal self-image is the reason loving yourself seems so incomprehensible. We are also bombarded with false messages in the media, from fearmongering nightly news to awful advertisements that tell us we need a product to be an adequate person worthy of love.

It's not your fault. Throughout your life, your mind has been conditioned to accept all the negativity surrounding you. Consider all the things that were said to us in childhood. Perhaps it was "You are lazy just like your Uncle Fred." Or maybe "You are so clumsy just like me." Or "You don't want to be rich because rich people are snobby and arrogant." No matter who said these things or how they said them, they have taken up space as deeply rooted beliefs about ourselves. We translate such comparisons and criticisms as "I am not good enough" and thereby limit our potential.

Some of us have been victims of different types of abuse that resulted in feelings of uselessness and unworthiness. We may feel unseen and unheard. From there, we may be programmed to spend the rest of our lives building a strong case against ourselves. It is difficult to reach a level of success when you are being internally sabotaged by thoughts of unworthiness, thoughts whose origins you cannot even place. Thoughts we have listened to and accepted as fact.

Is there anyone who has had a perfect childhood? I used to think so, back when I was at the comparing-myself-to-others stage, but now I know that even parents with the best intentions can be stressed and unable to handle child-rearing in keeping with the needs of the unique personality that was born through them. There are lessons for everyone from every type of household. There is no such thing as a perfect family—or perfect anything for that matter.

Everyone has been exposed to negative influences, both inside and outside the home, from teachers, friends, and relatives, who probably unintentionally or intentionally made us feel incomplete in some way. Subconscious programs we pick up along the way are running the show 95 percent of the time. Our behaviors reveal our unconscious belief that we are unlovable. We must unlearn what we have learned.

Your unconscious mind is so deeply programmed to see yourself in a negative light that it doesn't know anything different. Most of us look in the mirror and only see the things we want to change. That is just the physical aspect of ourselves. We are also good at feeling inadequate mentally by believing "I'm not smart enough." And if we think we are unlovable, we can come up short emotionally, too, and sabotage healthy relationships.

Your brain will lie to you to protect you, especially under stress. Remind yourself every day not to believe everything you think. Its just a thought. It doesn't mean it is a truth. Your mind will imagine worst-case scenarios so do not but into the negativity, or mean talk, or "should-ing" on yourself, and all the extreme ups or downs. Learn to be more open minded and flexible. Try to see some of the stuff your mind dreams up as funny and try a more lighthearted approach to your crazy thoughts. We can be hoodwinked by our primal minds, which are only trying to keep us safe—even when we are not in danger. It perceives change as dangerous, whereas we now know that change is *required* for better adaptation and growth to take place.

According to a fable from Hawaii, every child is born with a bowl filled with radiant light. Each child starts out as a shining, bright light. However, the bowl becomes heavier and darker as a child grows. This is because every time a child becomes resentful, a rock is placed into the bowl. If you feel envy and jealousy, another rock is added. Anger and fear are also rocks that dim the light in the bowl. We all acquire many rocks of our own that dim our light, and soon we become like a stone—solid, immovable, fixed, and hardened, unable to move with the grace, ease, and trust we once had. Letting go of residual resentment and blame is the answer. Blame is another rock blocking our light. The act of releasing blame also has a lightening up effect on your whole mind, body, and spirit, thus allowing easier access to your radiant bowl of self-love, your radiant bowl of light.

Unfortunately life is not always a bowl of cherries or a bowl of light. Instead we have placed some hard and heavy pits of residue from our experiences into our bowls. With awareness, we can look into our bowls and accept what is there, then empty the contents completely to restore, start fresh, and become the full spectrum of our own true radiance once again.

How do you do this exactly? It is mostly a "two steps forward and one step back" kind of process due to the injurious society we have been planted in. Using a meditation practice to regain peace and remain calm as we try and try again to love all of us. Love the rocks while you empty that bowl into an ocean of salty loving tears, and watch them dissolve one by one.

It really doesn't matter who programmed our psyche and when. Pinpointing the source of our deep-seated negative beliefs is not as important as claiming them now as our own. We have taken them on and must accept them to become responsible for our own health and happiness.

Your friends can help you with the process of revealing the negativity you carry around. I have given this privilege to the closest allies sharing my journey. Be careful who you share your revelations with, as there is a need for healthy boundaries when you are in a vulnerable position, and bullies can antagonize our efforts by adding to the unwanted negativity. I can't offer a formula for finding a trustworthy friendship except to rely on your intuition and follow a sympathetic energy with similar values. Someone that feels safe to be around and has stood the test of time with their supportive presence. When I put myself down, they pick up on the "other voice" that sounds like my mother. It is up to me to own my own voice now, the voice coming out of my mouth.

Awareness is key! Learn about yourself from every possible angle—from friends and from everyone you meet. You will hear yourself and often wonder where the heck that came from, or did I really mean to sound so mean? Start to recognize who is really doing the talking. Promise to *not* beat yourself up when you start to notice so many unloving things coming out. It is all part of the process. When you empty your bowl, you will feel lighter. But why wait? It is a lifelong procedure, you need to lighten up on yourself right now. It's OK to not take yourself so seriously. Think about it, most of the stuff isn't yours anyway. Have a laugh about it. Treat it as if you are cleaning out a closet and you find these weird clothes that don't fit and are out of fashion. Laugh at the silliness and smile at the fact you don't fit into that stuff anymore.

When I was in Bali, I loved the sound of the broom made from leaves they used every morning to sweep the path. It made the most wonderful, soft swooshing sound. Now I play that gentle sound in my mind whenever there is a subconscious cobweb that needs to be swept away.

Swoosh, swoosh. Swoosh, swoosh.

PRACTICE

Write down a negative belief as it appears in your mind. For example, "My boss hates me and always puts me down." Now pretend you are in a courtroom and it's time to build a case against this statement. Scan your memory until you find reasons to disprove the negative belief, such as "My boss actually gave me a compliment in the meeting last week."

Any time you notice self-talk that uses the words "always" or "never" or "should," be aware that these words are clues that lead to an untruth.

SELF-COMPASSION

You, yourself, as much as anybody in the entire universe deserve your love and affection.
—BUDDHA

Self-compassion is a process of being kind, supportive, and warm to yourself. It is the same as self-love, but it's not the same as self-esteem. Self-esteem is usually based on material possessions that build a false level of confidence that can slip away. If you feel better about yourself by constantly comparing, or bullying and putting down others, that is a false esteem that is contingent on often temporary outer circumstances.

Do not confuse self-compassion with narcissism and selfishness. Rather, look to the ancient wisdom of the Buddhists. Self-compassion is emphasized often in Buddhist teachings and can lead us to the steps we need to take toward loving ourselves with reverence. We want to value ourselves dearly with respect and high regard for being an amazing human being. That's it. You deserve your own admiration for no other reason than that you exist. Most people are brought up to believe they have to be constantly busy, work hard, make sacrifices, suffer, struggle, overachieve, gain notoriety, obtain riches and trappings of financial success, and look a certain way before they are deserving of their own love and appreciation.

The Metta meditation is especially helpful for accepting your love for yourself from yourself. Metta is an ancient term, similar to Sanskrit, from northern India; it means "positive energy and kindness toward others."

When I lead the classic Buddhist, loving-kindness (Metta) meditation, I often explain first that it is one of the four pillars of Buddhism—a noble attitude that frees one from suffering.

Buddha's visualization meditation increases empathy, compassion, and friendliness to yourself and others. This heart-opening exercise helps us to cultivate and build on our ability to give and receive compassion. It also encourages lightheartedness when we take ourselves and others too seriously, which is too often. I find it especially helpful for those with anxiety and feelings of overwhelming hopelessness—a condition that is at epidemic proportions due to the 24-hour news cycle, our addiction to social media, and the general state of world affairs. A changing world and the flux and flow of life is difficult to keep up with.

Meditation offers the helping hand we need to get off the roller coaster; when we shift our focus to extending well wishes to others, we not only become present but feel like we are not so helpless. We connect with the innate power of being of service. This intention enables us to contribute to society and release loving vibrations that add balance to a negative world and lift our spirits too.

Traditionally, meditators begin by bestowing this loving-kindness on themselves, but that can seem too much for Western minds to accept, so most meditation teachers begin with having you visualize someone you truly love and feel comfortable around; you visualize them sitting in front of you, and say their name silently, beginning the Metta phrases.

Any combination or similar verbiage to the following will work:

> May you be happy.
> May you be healthy.

May you be safe.
May you be peaceful.
May you be loved.

This is a great way to get the love flowing and ease into the practice.

Then we bring to mind a neutral person, which means an acquaintance we only see occasionally, like a pharmacist or delivery person.

Next, we take a deep breath because it's time to bring to mind a difficult person who pushes your buttons and ruffles your feathers. We all have one; it could be a bully, a family member, a friend, or quite often, a politician.

Finally, it is your turn to receive your own loving-kindness. I ask my class to bring to mind something special about themselves that they love. There must be something you like about yourself that makes you unique, even if it is something simple or a talent. It is not a crime to feel pride and approval for yourself, so once you get those feel-good feelings for yourself flowing, you say either out loud or silently to yourself the above phrases, adding at the end, "May I be loved unconditionally by me."

Lastly, but most importantly, it is time to spread this love to the world and say "May *all* beings be happy, healthy, safe, peaceful, and loved."

Self-compassion is a powerful, positive energy that is necessary for a healthy balance between mind, body, and spirit. When you are full of self-compassion, you have something genuine to share with the world, and when you believe you are worthy, others will see your value and your life will reflect it. Your internal happiness will have outer consequences. You will finally believe you are enough. Enough to achieve anything you set your mind to that makes the world a better place. You deserve to be happy, and you can believe this on a deep, profound level. Now you have happiness to share.

The true immensity of speaking to yourself with more kindness and patience is that when you begin to be kinder and judge yourself less, it creates a space for more compassion toward others. I personally enjoy using these phrases mentally toward others during a crowded commute, in a tense grocery line, or anywhere a stress-release valve could come in handy. It has helped in miraculous ways to diffuse a situation when I've been trapped on the tarmac in an airplane or traveling in strange places with a language barrier.

What we are striving for is loving ourselves unconditionally exactly the same way we love our children and pets. Too often, instead, we love ourselves with conditions. We expect to be happy only when we get the job we want, or only after acquiring something new or finding that perfect soulmate or losing weight, for example. Then and only then do we feel worthy of our self-compassion. Let's turn this around and make sure those things we desire are actually worthy of us!

Even when we attain those outside circumstances, often the happiness is temporary. Trying to control and manipulate the outside hasn't really worked out for us, has it? So now we need to make some changes from the inside out, especially if we are prone to perfectionism.

Eckhart Tolle said, "Get the inside right, and the outside will fall into place." Inside is where our love waits for us. If that sounds easier and less exhausting than the way we have been chasing perfection, that's because it is.

It is impossible to love yourself unconditionally while still being a control freak. Micromanagers lack peace in their lives. We all know someone, or we have these tendencies ourselves and wish we could just chill out and accept change a little more easily. When dealing with mounting stress, the controllers try even harder to get results, yet this creates more pressure.

It is unrealistic to expect to control everything that happens to us today and in the days to come, yet so many of us feel extreme anxiety over getting every detail just right and defining a particular outcome. This will exacerbate negative thoughts.

Bulldozing your way through life leaves little room for self-compassion. This is spiraling behavior: we give ourselves unrealistic challenges and set ourselves up for a failure that we can then use to denigrate ourselves even further. If this sounds at all familiar, it is time to try a more flexible approach.

Why does everything on the outside have to be so perfect? Are we feeling out of control on the inside? Control is a reaction to fear; fear of what will happen if we don't get the result we are pushing so hard for.

This is exhausting for ourselves and the people around us. The problem arises when we get caught up in overthinking and focusing on what will go wrong without weighing what could go right. As Franklin D. Roosevelt so aptly stated, "The only thing we have to fear is fear itself."

There are ways to let go of clutching and clinging to a my-way-or-the-highway attitude. Attaining more peace requires you to lighten up on yourself and others. Loosen the reigns and see how many more options start to appear for you. These apply to the most mundane decisions we make as well as the major life changers.

Studies have shown that the stress response can be triggered by the "perception" of a threat, even when there is no reality of danger. If it is really all in our minds, then there is hope for the over-controllers, because a thought can be changed.

Every one of your thoughts is creating your future, and life will follow each thought to flow toward a positive or a negative experience. It is all in how you look at it; the choice is yours. To be optimistic and live in a happy, friendly world, you must stop controlling and micromanaging every detail.

"The mental suffering you create," says Eckhart Tolle, "is always some form of non-acceptance, some form of unconscious resistance to what is. The intensity of the suffering depends on the degree of resistance to the present moment." Next time you feel that you are losing control of a situation because fighting to change the outer circumstances isn't working, you can choose to experience the same situation—only differently. Observing it from another perspective is something you can control. Instead of blaming something or someone else, you can accept it wholeheartedly for what it is. We must all learn to do this without judgment or opinion.

When you change the way you look at things, the things themselves can begin to change too. You can choose to shift your reality from worry and fear to peace and love.

Change is good and necessary for spiritual growth.

In the wise words of Napoleon Hill, "Through the law of change, man is forced to keep on growing." Hill believed that we must have flexible personalities in order to grow.

Next time someone offers to go to a restaurant you previously refused to go to, or offers to drive instead, or picks the movie for the night, you can choose to just go with it and relax in order to prove that the outcome will work out for the best without your constant input. Feel good about allowing others to take the wheel.

An attitude of gratitude slows down the impulse to alter and control a situation. Studies of people keeping a gratitude journal report an increase in alertness, enthusiasm, energy, and goal attainment. They feel better about their lives as a whole and are more optimistic about the coming week. Even without a journal, just recalling one different thing a day you can be grateful for will make you less fearful of the future, making it easier to relinquish control.

Deepak Chopra advises us to let go of rigid ideas on how things "should be," and to remain open for new opportunities. This constitutes Chopra's sixth spiritual law of success, the law of detachment. Otherwise we are just limiting our own future. What we need is to get out of our own way. After all, how do we really know what is going to be best out of all the amazing possibilities the world has to offer? Let go and open yourself to the natural flow of the universe.

Without meditation, stress will activate the control freak in you, and will choose the black over the white, meaning it will exaggerate false flaws or past failures rather than believing your strengths and achievements. Optimism is a choice, and meditation is a gateway. Optimism comes easier when you are in a relaxed state.

But meditation is more than a method of stress relief; it is also the great shifter of perception. "Through training our minds," the Dalai Lama suggests, "with constant effort, we can change our mental perceptions or mental attitudes. This can make a real difference in our lives. If we have a positive mental attitude, then even when surrounded by hostility, we shall not lack inner peace."

The pursuit of perfection is exhausting and wearing on mind, body, and soul. We need to let go of the idea of being flawless. Let's agree right now that we are all perfectly imperfect and in a state of constant change and evolution. Change is good and flexibility is a necessity for nurturing self-compassion.

In the *Tao Te Ching*, Lao Tzu says,

> [A]n army without flexibility never wins a battle.
> A tree that is unbending is easily broken.
> The hard and strong will fall.
> The soft and weak will overcome.

Another quote, from the Buddha, is one you can say over and over until it sinks in: "You, yourself, as much as anybody in the entire universe, deserve your love and affection." Now let's say it this way together, three times: I deserve my love and affection. I deserve my love and affection. I deserve my love and affection.

Verbalizing these words, and writing them down as many times as you need to, will reinforce your commitment and desire for change and send a clear message to the brain and subconscious mind that you are setting up a new mindset and are ready to alter your perception from fear and loathing to the highest vibration of all—unconditional love for ourselves.

Yes! It makes perfect sense. Why wouldn't you deserve compassion both for and from yourself? I love the way Buddha says "just as much as anyone in the universe." It reminds me of how we give and give and give so willingly to our jobs, family, friends, and community. There seems to be no limit to our giving for others. We can be proud of our contributions. Caring and volunteering is wonderful and feels good for a while, but does it leave you feeling depleted, exhausted by always placing yourself at the bottom of the list?

Don't forget about *you*. You *do* have a right to feel loving-kindness for your wonderful self, just as much as everyone you care for does. You deserve your love just for being you.

PRACTICE

Listen to my "Compassion" track on the *Tranquil Me* app to experience a Metta meditation. Check out Sharon Salzburg, a Buddhist Metta expert who brought this visualization meditation to the West. Her awesome books on mindfulness and compassion are well worth your time.

11

LETTING GO

Don't wait for the perfect moment. Take the moment and make it perfect.
—BUDDHA

Remember my story about the time I stopped recording my voice as a teenager? There are many other instances in my life where I believed what others said to me and accepted it as truth. No doubt there are many in your life. We all want to be "normal" and to "fit in," to be like everyone else or just do as we are told to be a good person. Early on, we start covering up and hiding our talents and passionate interests. Leaning into who we are and our uniqueness is all too often discouraged at a very young age. How many of us were stifled by a blanket of blandness, of obedience, accepting the opinions of others on how your life should be.

Looking back as adults, we can see that even with good intentions these negative influencers had their own issues and probably don't even remember what they said. Most people are self-obsessed, trapped in their own limited world, unaware of the hurt they can inflict with a simple statement or observation that makes us feel that we are wrong or not enough in some way.

Yes, by now it's history, and as much as we'd like to sometimes, we can't change it. But we can stop our history from controlling our behavior by reframing the past so the effect it has on us in the present and future will be more realistic and loosen its destructive hold over us.

When we do a postmortem on a deep wound, it has an incredible healing effect on our perception and, therefore, our capacity to see beauty. So I recommend trying to identify a particular moment you are holding on to, and even more than one if possible. But the first moment that pops into your head is the best place to start. It will provide clarity on why you do what you do and can explain where a self-defeating pattern came from.

This is your chance to turn your wounds into wisdom. It allows you to learn and grow and move forward with a new attitude. Prepare to dive deep in order to unravel your past so the future can shine brighter. Together we will rip off the Band-Aid and truly heal the past once and for all. Then we can leave it where it belongs—in the past.

Reframing a story does not mean rewriting history; it means stepping back and viewing it from a wider angle, and seeing details that allow us to understand where our thinking became distorted regarding the incident. It is our *thinking* that continues to hurt us, not the event itself!

This exercise will give us a chance to learn something new from the past and to let go of it. Say that from the original event we learned we were lacking in some way and unworthy of praise. But looking back, it becomes clear that it was the best we could do at the time. Now we are ready to accept the truth of the situation and learn that we were fine as we were. This knowledge helps us move forward and shifts those inner blocks.

PRACTICE

Take the time to write down your story. It is vital to put pen to paper or fingers to keyboard. Writing it out will sort out all those crazy thoughts and help you see the memories in a way that reveals that they are just thoughts. Not all thoughts are a fact. Get them out of your head and just begin with whatever comes to mind first.

Use the following prompts:

> What happened?
> How did you feel?
> Who was there?
> Where were you?
> What was said?
> How did you both behave?

You may find that this reveals triggers that can bring back the hurt and highlight any buttons that can be pushed by others. It is also extremely helpful to identify a piece of sensory information that can be associated with the incident in question. Maybe the smell of your father's ashtray or your mother's soap. This awareness can change your reactions under stress in the future.

Just write as much as you can and take as long as you need to get it out, using as much detail as possible. One child's mild discipline can be considered a cruel punishment to another. This is a private moment between you and you. No need to show what you write to anyone. It is just for your own emotional release.

The benefits of written purging are well documented, and I hope these benefits motivate you to complete this essential task. It will have a positive physical effect, such as an increase in immunity, greater resilience to stress, and an improvement in mood, to name a few.

Look at the incident you are summoning from the past objectively. See where the confusion can become clarity. Discover something within that discomfort. Do this with compassion and patience and without judgment. You aren't opening this old wound to simply press on it until it hurts. Rather, you want to learn from it so it can be released and you can move forward without the pain getting in the way of your love and the decisions you make daily. When you finally let go of the rope to your past, you will create a sense of relief and a lightness of being like never before.

You may be limiting your life right now with a belief you have had since you were a little kid. Think about what you used to believe when you were small. Place these false beliefs about yourself into the same delete folder where you have put the Easter Bunny and Santa Claus. When I was six years old, I really believed there were eight days a week because of the Beatles song on the radio!

Childhood sadness may still be shaping your everyday life, but once you face it, you can unlatch the shutters obstructing your view of the world. It's time to open the windows, take a deep breath, and let the light of love shine in.

PRACTICE

Journal what you think you needed from your parents but didn't receive. Was it approval? Interest? Affection? Make a list and a plan of how you can give these things to yourself. List the basic human needs you only focused on providing for others and instead will now focus on yourself. Sleep, companionship, hydration, hunger, spirituality, mental and emotional needs—how will you meet these?

HEARTS BREAK OPEN

There is no path to happiness. Happiness is the path.
—BUDDHA

A broken heart is an opportunity for a time out and to fall in love with your true authentic self. You need to get into a better place before you enter into another relationship, even while nurturing your relationship with yourself. Place all wounds and all feelings out into the light of loving and kind awareness. Hold yourself with care and forgiveness for healing peace to surface.

Think of it as if you are in a bad romance—but with yourself. You can go from loathing to loving yourself beginning with baby steps of "self-like" by starting a daily meditation practice that connects you to a place of peace and love waiting within.

Are you ready for a fresh start? Open the window to let in the fresh breeze of possibilities and allow positive energy to flow through your heart and mind. Your soul has led you to this place of peace. Listen to its whispers of invitation to a beautiful landscape that can only be found inside. The soul that came into this world as you is beckoning you within, where all the beauty of the ages lives inside—as you. Once there, your outer life will reflect that same beauty because your love is revealed and—finally—seen by you.

Now is exactly the time for a new relationship—with yourself. While you heal and get to the place where you are ready for another relationship, consider having a love affair with your amazing, genuine, unique self without the neediness of the perfect outside conditions in order to be happy. Dedicate time by yourself to not just grieve but to heal. Healing means to be alone with yourself and face the harsh realities you have been avoiding by jumping into relationships before learning the lesson from the previous dependency, and using that experience for self-growth and deep reflection. The dopamine addiction from the attention of that person you were attached to can now be turned around to heal you. You can discover what you need to give yourself in order to meet your needs and desires, all by yourself. Yes, you can be truly fulfilled with your own company. Your best friend is you and is craving quality time.

When you find your own happiness and someone comes along who is attracted by that loving glow of contentment, they can bask in that glow. Then, like a pair of happy little lightning bugs, you can enjoy the fun and friendship while lighting up the world.

You cannot recognize the love in others until you begin to love yourself. That may explain why we sometimes sabotage potential loving situations whether consciously or subconsciously. Some of the blame for enabling our feeling a lack of love comes from unrealistic romantic movies. Remember that no one else needs to "complete" you once you are already whole and have everything you need for love and success just as you are.

An initial step is to accept that you are not broken, even though you may have a broken heart, that there is nothing about you that needs to be fixed. If your heart has been broken open, what can you do? I suggest that you can allow the walls you have built around it to fall away so that, rather than falling in love on the rebound, you can fall in love with yourself with more than enough love left over for another. Release the need to criticize and blame yourself for the end of a special relationship. It is still special because of the wonderful lessons it taught you about yourself.

So you see, it is actually more about letting go of what no longer serves you than it is about adding something you think is missing. It's about discovery of the treasure hidden in the rubble of false beliefs that are reinforced by cultural influences such as movies and social media.

My codependency and shame issues became clear after I had hit my head against so many brick walls (in the form of men) that I was finally forced to face everything I was repressing and hiding about my past traumas. The decisions I had been making, I realized, came from a place of projecting my abandonment issues, shame, and deep childhood wounds onto some unsuspecting guy who was attracted to something else altogether—qualities I was unable to see in myself because of my low self-worth. I had been valuing myself as much as a worthless chipped coffee mug at a garage sale that no one wanted!

This led to my choosing unavailable or toxic relationships. Nice guys were rarely interested in putting up with my moods, and frankly, they were always "too nice" for my taste. I didn't believe I deserved to be treated nicely. I was usually found chasing the players. A classic codependent, I used every emotionally unavailable guy I was attracted and attached to as a chance to perpetuate my belief that I was unlovable.

Studying the issues, I was shocked to find how prevalent codependency is among all ages and genders. Among the symptoms are low self-esteem, people-pleasing, and obsessive thinking. My advice is to research codependency for yourself to see if it is a topic you can dive into. Investigate all the studies which point to recovery and healing as a definite possibility. Two good places to start are *Codependency for Dummies* by Darlene Lancer and Melody Beattie's *Codependent No More*.

A prerequisite to falling in love with yourself is to "Know Thyself," which is inscribed on the Temple of Apollo in ancient Greece. I mean *all* of thyself! There is a part of us I call the inner critic or the victim. The critic is why we sabotage our romances—and yes, we all self-sabotage.

Once I realized that my subconscious was running the show, I understood how I had pushed away and rejected the good relationships so I could wallow in self-pity like a classic victim, which only perpetuates our deep beliefs of unworthiness. You might feel blame and anger toward the inner critic and the victim, and symbolically want to duct tape and throw these characters over a bridge like in a gangster movie, but even they need love.

Unleashing the healing power of love is to bring kind understanding to these parts of ourselves that were first conceived to protect us from hurt. Like your pain-body, once you see them for what they are, they will shrink in importance and have less impact on your decisions and attitudes. They will merely be diminishing echoes of an old wound. Time won't heal old wounds without self-acceptance, awareness, compassion, and loving discipline; these will allow you to grow into the greatest version of yourself. You will know that you are getting close to this place of peace when you find there is wisdom in those wounds and they light up the path to your own tender heart.

PRACTICE

Draw a picture of your inner saboteurs as people. Stick figures or cutting out an image from a magazine or finding something from the internet will do. Give them names—maybe Judge Jenny or Vicky the Victim—and start to recognize when they show up. Talk to them, tell them they can go sit in the corner. Their self-talk and ideas are obsolete and cannot help this new optimistic, wiser version of you. This will give you a chance to breathe and gather yourself so you can respond appropriately instead of with the usual knee-jerk negative reaction.

Romance yourself—first and foremost with the same loving attention you would lavish on that person who you suppose will fulfill your every desire. And replace those expectations with a reality check. Hope and happiness patiently await you at the end of your rocky road to romance. You are fine as you are and don't need a serious relationship to validate your worth.

Denial is the first thing that must go for any of this work to take root. Denial about the painful reality in your relationships, denial about your past, and denial of your feelings, needs, and codependency.

Take it from my experience, approaching a love relationship from a place of lack and desperation or neediness is a perfect storm for impending drama and suffering that projects fear instead of love to the other. After all, how can you truly love if you don't realize that you are a being of love, living a life of love? The ever-quotable Wayne Dyer put it like this: "You can't give away what you don't have."

As far back as 350 BC, Aristotle wrote that "self-love is a prerequisite to loving others." So what we are talking about is not a cringey, new age hashtag. Loving yourself means respecting yourself and opening up your heart for a bigger, more satisfying love instead of a small space kept for the tiny crumbs thrown in your direction. We all need to stop fooling ourselves and stop ignoring our need for true, unconditional love.

If there is a shortage of "me-love" in your life, there will be less "we-love" to give to a partner. A half a heart can only fill another heart halfway. If you carry contempt because of a bad breakup, that is what you will be giving away. You get back from the world what you give out.

That is why forgiveness is essential always—*especially* after a breakup. It is a powerful practice that will change your life and clear the path for a loving soul to enter. It is a gift to yourself, not to the person you think wronged you! It is for your benefit alone. Holding onto anger and resentment has no effect on the other person, but it will harm you. And living without blame or judgment frees up more space for love. Start moving from a victim mentality to a state of knowing that you can actually have anything you want. Maybe it's time to ask "What do *I* want?" Journal and figure it out. When you are ready to start over, knowing you can achieve anything you put your mind to, the world becomes new, replenished.

Are we ready to empty our suitcase of romantic fairy-tale expectations and limitations that are getting in the way of our happiness? Yes we are! Let's unpack the craziness we collected thus far and clean up our act so we don't have to carry it to the next relationship.

According to Marianne Williamson in *A Return to Love*, every relationship is a divine assignment and a call to love—a lesson. We need to stop filling our luggage with resentment and blame, and instead choose to unpack our emotional baggage before we dump it onto the next person of interest. You then create a space for new energy to flow and a fresh beginning to unfold.

After a breakup is the perfect time to transform the pain, loss, anger, sadness, and confusion into a creative energy that can be used to fuel a life of self-love with new healthy boundaries, new ways to relate to yourself and then others. Use this time alone to look at the relational patterns you may be stuck in. What a perfect time to break a pattern that no longer serves you.

It is possible to see where we were codependent and clingy without blame or self-loathing. It is time to own it all in order to let it all go. You will begin your next relationship with relief and with freedom from illusion, self-sacrifice, and suffering. You will be truly free to be your authentic lovable self, open for the love you so much deserve.

Let's get ready to enjoy the power that comes with authenticity. You can be happy right now, with or without a romantic partner. Learn to cherish, pamper, and truly love your true self, to love from the inside out. You no longer need to wait for those three words to come out of someone else's mouth as proof of your worthiness. *You* can say "I love you" in the mirror or as you meditate on your open heart.

Broken hearts are exacerbated by love songs and, especially, breakup songs. Once again our culture of romantic rubbish finds a way to make us feel like losers. So next time you hear your favorite love song and it reminds you of the person who let you down (remember, you were a different person with low self-esteem when you attracted that type), look on it as a moment of relapse—you are missing the drama, and longing for the brief moments of affection like an addict.

When that feeling of sadness (often just out of habit) starts to rise to the surface and that lump in your throat appears, this time you will know what is happening and will be a little more objective while remaining in awareness of the feelings you are feeling. You don't want to repress it, but do look at it for what it is without diving into the murky depths of despair or victimhood.

But you can still listen to that song, because I have a tried and tested tip for turning that frown upside down! Sing the song to yourself and answer the song. This is practical and easy. I change the words to suit my self-love. When Linda Ronstadt sings "When will I be loved?" tell her "Right now, by me!"

Music is a powerful shifter of consciousness. It will instantly change the way you feel and, as we all know from the cycle of self-loathing, that converts thoughts and then behavior. Music is used to manipulate us when we are being entertained. Movies and TV series would be lost without the important element music provides in communicating to an audience the intentions for a scene.

By the first few bars in the opening few minutes, we instantly know if the backdrop is romantic or mysterious. Use music to help you get in touch with the finer, more subtle vibrations that can lift and enlighten you.

According to research into hit songs, they have found that they have one thing in common: the beat mimics the natural rhythm of the heart. Our heart beat then mimics back and aligns with whatever song we are listening to. This is a reminder to be aware of your environment and what you consume. You absorb and ingest more than food. Make sure your environment is enriching you too. People, media and even music can have a healthy influence.

Fake it until that love vibration becomes a familiar part of who you are and is easier to access when you need it. Let us not fall, but rise in love—love for ourselves above and beyond the drama and ego suffering.

Below is a selection of empowering tunes to get you feeling good. You can find these songs and many others on a curated playlist to accompany this book. Go to Spotify and find Kathryn Remati Befriend Yourself self love playlist.

> "I Am Light" (India.Arie); "Who You Are" (Jesse J); "Thank You, Next" (Arianna Grande); "Holiday" (Madonna); "Born This Way" (Lady Gaga); "Beautiful" (Christina Aguilera); "Stronger" (Kelly Clarkson); "Good as Hell" (Lizzo); "Brand New Day" (Van Morrison); "The Greatest Love" (Whitney Houston); "Perfect" (Pink); "Fight Song" (Rachel Platten); "Girl on Fire" (Alicia Keys); "Just Fine" (Mary J. Blige); "Respect" (Aretha Franklin); "Love Myself" (Hailee Steinfeld); "Feeling Myself" (Nicki

Minaj and Beyonce); "I Can" (Nas); "Firework" (Katie Perry); "Stronger Woman" (Jewel); "Video" (India.Arie); "Feelin' Good" (Nina Simone); "Let Me Blow Ya Mind" (Eve and Gwen Stefani); "All About That Bass" (Meghan Trainor); "Who Says" (Selena Gomez); "Ray of Light" (Madonna).

You can also feed your soul with inspirational music, such as Indian devotional chanting or yoga and meditation music. Combining listening with mindful movement, such as yoga or tai chi, is a centering and uplifting way to flood your system with divine love.

I recommend the Saul David Raye album *Ten Thousand Suns* and the song "Fall in Love with God." Another appropriate and healing album is *Sacred Music for a Broken Heart* by Mirabai Ceiba, notably the song "In Dreams." I like to do my yoga to Ben Leinbach songs, such as "Radiance Prayer to Goddess Saraswati." Other favorites are the Steve Ross albums of mantras *Grace* and *Give Love a Chants Live* Or simply ask Alexa to play Deva Primal Radio on Pandora.

PRACTICE

Write a love letter to yourself.

Here is where you finally get to hear the words you have been longing for. Keep this letter and work on it over time, adding to it as your self-discovery grows and you realize maybe there is even more you can say that is loving. Have a loving one-way conversation that makes sure you know that you are appreciated and loved.

You can read your letter whenever you need to get back on track, when the self-doubt drops by. Rereading what you have written will be a wonderful reminder of your worth and goodness!

13

SELF-FORGIVENESS

Forgiveness is a gift to yourself.
—BUDDHA

Accepting yourself exactly as you are right now as well as everything in your past will have an enormous impact on every aspect of your life.

And now that we have realized there is no one to blame and that everyone else is doing the best they can, it is time to self-forgive, which is a key part of befriending and loving ourselves.

First, try to be aware of when you are replaying all the memories that have hurt you and keep hurting you all over again. Next, ask what it is that you have found so unforgivable about yourself. Did you do or say something that you wish you hadn't? (Innocence or guilt does not matter in this context.) Forgiveness of others releases us from the past and lightens our load, freeing us from the heaviness of hate. Forgiveness of yourself is equally essential.

Mistakes are a prerequisite to any life. You might see your past as a long string of mistakes, but I believe there are no mistakes, because all experiences, whether we label them as good or bad, give us the knowledge and expertise we need to reach our highest potential and be equipped for our dharma or calling to our life of service. You are who you are right now as a result of every decision you ever made.

Mistakes are just a kind of experience, and experiences are for learning and growing, not for punishment. So stop judging yourself. Would you judge a dear friend so harshly? No.

No matter what harm you think you did, you can forgive yourself and move on. Let's leave it in the past where it belongs. Whatever it is, it's over. Quit carrying it around, ruining the present and sabotaging your future.

To illustrate this point, I like to tell the story of two Buddhist monks. They are out walking, and they have to cross a stream. But they find a scared woman trapped on one side. So the older monk picks her up and takes her across. Then the two monks continue down the road. After a while, the young monk scolds the older one, asking why he picked her up when they are not supposed to interact physically with women. The older monk replies, "I put her down miles ago; why are you still carrying her?"

What are *you* still carrying around mentally and emotionally that is blocking your peace and appreciation of this very moment? Putting down instead of carrying means to let go of the idea of perfection and accepting that no one is perfect or infallible, and that removing expectations of yourself and others will lighten your life in wondrous ways.

One powerful way to release past burdens and affect reconciliation with yourself is the Ho'oponopono Hawaiian forgiveness ritual practiced by traditional indigenous healers and psychologists. To perform that ritual yourself, visualize sitting in front of yourself or look into a mirror. Now say aloud or silently to yourself:

> I'm sorry.
> Please forgive me.
> Thank you.
> I love you.

Now, again, with sincerity and compassion, as you hug yourself with your eyes closed or looking directly into a mirror with a hand on your heart, say to yourself:

> I'm sorry.
> Please forgive me.
> Thank you.
> I love you.
> I'm sorry, I'm sorry, I'm sorry.
> Please forgive me, please forgive me, please forgive me.
> Thank you, thank you, thank you.
> I love you, I love you, I love you.

This exercise has had miraculous results for clearing karma from this life and past lives. It is a method of self-forgiveness that, along with the following affirmations, will help you escape from the chains of your past. You can lighten up, reclaim, and reset for a brighter lighter future.

AFFIRMATIONS

- I approve of myself.
- I love myself unconditionally.
- I release the past and let it go.
- I move forward with love.
- It is safe to love and forgive myself just as I am.
- I accept all parts of me, the messy and the neat.
- I learn from all my experiences.
- I am always doing the best I can.
- I forgive myself and others easily.
- I am enough.
- Love is everywhere.
- I am forgiven.
- I am blessed.
- I release the need to be perfect.

- I love all of me.
- I deserve to have love and forgiveness in my life.
- I am choosing love and forgiveness for myself.
- My heart is open for love to flow through me and to me.
- I did the best I could.
- I am lighthearted as I release the burdens of my past.
- I befriend myself.
- Every single experience, no matter how I label it—good, bad, tragic, or toxic—teaches me valuable lessons.
- I love the way I learn from all my experiences.
- I trust myself.
- I deserve forgiveness.
- I am forgiven by me.
- My mind, body, and spirit are lighter and brighter.
- I am forgiving myself unconditionally now and forever.
- I am grateful for every new day, a fresh start, and a chance to begin again with forgiveness in my heart.
- I am exactly where I am supposed to be right now.

We all came to this planet for a reason: to touch the hearts of others. Most of the time we are unaware of the impact we have had, and will have, on everyone whose paths we cross.

Fully experiencing your emotions is important, and greater awareness will prevent them from morphing into unproductive self-pity that can only serve to keep you stuck in the past. Wallowing in self-loathing increases suffering and holds you back from the brighter future just around the corner.

While it is OK to feel feelings fully even in our darkest moments of sadness and lonely unworthiness, we can do so without buying into the idea of unworthiness as a truth. As meditators, we have learned not to believe everything we think; the same idea applies to everything we feel. Emotions are also temporary in nature, and each one will soon be replaced with another feeling. Let them come and go without attaching a false belief or distorted thought to it. The distorted thinking comes from our place of past pain.

Let me slow down here and say that I don't want to sound flippant, as if an attitudinal adjustment is so easy. It is not easy. In fact, darkness is an integral part of the journey to lightness of heart and mind. Remember, our aim is to have unconditional love, which includes unconditional acceptance and forgiveness for every part of ourselves. So instead of hiding your shadowy, dark side, like a ghost in an attic, bring it out into the light of tender awareness.

If you learn to love your dark side, it become less spooky, and when it comes back to haunt you, you can apply a color to the emotion—maybe angry red or depressing black. Even give it shape and character if you wish. Speak to it: "Hello, old friend. I see you are looking a little gray tonight, and it's OK to be here for a while. I get why you are triggered and it's cool, so I will enjoy some self-care and maybe take a walk and take some deep breaths." Once you are accepting of your lower emotions, you can break up energetically with unhealthy patterns. You can open yourself up to the positive ones that have been limited in their range. When you cap any emotion, it blocks the love too. For example, when you see repressed anger as another brick in that wall you built around your heart, it is easier to dissolve it in the light of acceptance. It then follows that the other more pleasurable emotions of joy and ecstasy can be reached. It's hard to connect to someone else's heart when your heart is being muffled. Eventually, with love, the ghosts of the painful past will fade away as ghosts do when the sun of forgiveness comes out.

Remember that emotions and experiences are neither good nor bad. They are just another mystical and fantastic ingredient that makes us who we are. I like to think of our lives as a big pot of soup. You are like a unique recipe, brimming with goodness from all the ingredients that bring their own flavor to the mix.

It's true that some experiences may be bitter, but others are sweet. Till now, you may have hesitated to add certain elements to the mix because you think of them as toxic and poisonous to the soup. But that is not possible! The broth is a magical elixir that turns all experiences, whether traumatic, romantic, painful, or dreadfully unfair, into a delicious, heartwarming fusion that makes you who you are.

It is safe to throw your wounds, heartbreaks, salty tears, and depression into the pot. Instead of thinking of yourself as a messy, yucky plate of moldy memories and scraps of ugly untruths, picture yourself as a heavenly bowl of delectable, flavorful stew.

The broth is a divine light or soul that we all have in common. As children, we began as a consommé of calm curiosity, and like a five-star chef, our life experience has prepped us for an authentic, organic, delicious, homegrown recipe that originates from wherever you are on this planet.

Our outer identities reflect the kind of soup we are. And peeling back the layers of ingredients that go into the different kinds of soup is what makes the world so full of flavor. You may be a curry, a gumbo, a chowder, a French bisque, or a hearty porridge. Whether pureed, smooth, or chunky, the soups are all palatable, and each has its own zest to add to the world. Experiment and try other soups, knowing that each recipe is a hodgepodge of goodness made from the same heavenly stock.

Love your heartwarming soup, and enjoy how the flavors mix so beautifully. Have some and be assured that loving your particular flavor is why you are able to share it so willingly and without conditions. Think to yourself: "Try my soup! It will warm your heart. I know it will because it warms mine every day."

There is plenty of savory soup to share. Don't worry about splashing it around. Just keep stirring the pot and mixing it up. The cup is always overflowing with loving nourishment that feeds not only your soul but many other lucky souls. As long as you are alive, you will have a pot on the stove of life simmering away, ready for the next ingredient to be added. How grateful are you right now that you have a pot? It means you are alive!

Next time you are in the dark cloud of despair, remind yourself, "I am in the goop"—the soupy mix you find inside a cocoon. The magical stuff that turns a caterpillar into a butterfly. Your loving awareness has brought you to this place of transition. The darkness is where the seeds of potential are buried, where transformation happens. It won't last forever, so it's OK to get a little excited, because your wings are on their way.

PRACTICE

At least once a day, look into your own eyes in a mirror and say "I love you." Notice the color and the emotion in your eyes. Mindfully, without judgment, say into your soul "I love you," and see reflected back at you the beauty, sweetness, and innocence that a lover or loving parent would see when looking into the windows to your beautiful soul. This is a transcendent and powerful way to increase your self-compassion.

14

GRATITUDE

Happiness will never come to those who fail to appreciate what they already have.
—BUDDHA

Thanksgiving is an American holiday when family reunions occur, and as the traditional turkey is being carved, guests in turn are asked, "What are you thankful for?" One day a year is better than nothing to count your blessings, but just imagine how much richer and happier your life would be if you answered that question on a daily basis! Let's take the Dalai Lama's advice: "Wake up saying every day is precious." It is never too late to incorporate a gratitude practice into our daily routine.

Gratitude researcher Dr. Robert Emmett defines gratefulness as "a life orientation to noticing and appreciating all the positive in the world." It is a coping skill that will get us out of the rut of compulsive complaining that prevents us from seeing the beauty and goodness that is always right in front of us. A gratitude practice is a daily acknowledgment of the many miracles that surround us that we take for granted.

In *Awakening the Buddha Within*, Lama Surya Das tells us that the "wonder, surprise, and possibility in each moment whether the experience is unpleasant, pleasant, or neutral, must be met as 'wonder-full.'"

Simply the act of writing about positive experiences has been associated with increased physical health and well-being and with being at the receiving end of help from others. Mental health also is improved due to a shift from negativity to gratitude in the form of positive thinking. If all we see is what is wrong with "this picture," then our brain gets the message that we want more of the same, and next thing you know, you are in a rut of constantly complaining about all the woes of the world. This is particularly important for anyone addicted to the 24-hour news cycle, full of disastrous weather and political mayhem, that feeds your fears. Turn it off. Turn off the news. Give yourself a break and your worst-case-scenario mind can be free to find things in the world to be grateful for instead. This can change your energetic vibration, which in turn affects the pulse of the planet. Just research quantum physics and read *The Biology of Belief* by Bruce Lipton for more details.

Gratitude reverses that negative mode of operating. The brain starts to focus on more of what we like than what we don't like. Choosing to feed your brain with complaints will only attract more of what you don't want. Instead, choose to look for more of what you *do* want. Things you need and want will start showing up.

It is a very simple equation. As Einstein said, "You are only confined by the walls you build yourself." This opens the pathways to more peace, more goodness, more beauty, and more appreciation for the good things that are always there right in front of us yet go unnoticed and get taken for granted. It bears repeating that what you appreciate, appreciates! Happiness really is an inside job.

There are hundreds of modern neuroscientific studies that show gratitude leading to a rise in oxytocin, dopamine, and serotonin, thus proving a biological "elevation of enjoyment" (Desmond Tutu), including during difficult situations. So even though we may feel hardwired for a life of suffering, there actually is a way to cultivate this elusive feeling of joy.

According to the Mayo Clinic, a daily gratitude practice "can increase happiness by 25 percent." It can "boost your energy, improve your mood, generate optimism, increase your well-being, help you bounce back faster, enhance self-esteem, make you kinder, improve your connections, decrease your risk of alcoholism, help you sleep better, help you recover more quickly from illness, boost your immunity, decrease your risk of infections, and even help you make more money."

Gratitude brings contentment and has also been known to attract the flow of good fortune and success our way.

It can provide essential insight needed for goal achievement, helping you arrive at your end result in a rapid manner. When you are focused on what you want, you are sure to receive it faster than you would if you see nothing but problems and hurdles in your way. Turn a problem into a project by giving it a different label and a different perspective. To return to Einstein: "We cannot solve a problem with the same thinking that created it."

I am a firm believer in building attitudinal muscle through gratitude. Get more of the "can do" thoughts working for you. Whether you choose to think it is possible or not, you are going to prove yourself to be correct. So why not just give it a try. Have you ever met someone that left you feeling blah and you could only give a vague description of them as having "a bad attitude?" Gratitude will make sure someone else is not describing you like that. Be the type of person others are attracted to and reach out to because their vulnerability feels safe with your positive and kind perspective of life. As Maya Angelou said, "Be the rainbow in someone else's cloud." Validate; support with hope and gratitude. Be that way for yourself first so you can be a light for others.

Also, since feeling gratefulness fills your life with appreciation and acceptance for what is right in front of you, wishing for what someone else has will be less frequent. We need to stop comparing ourselves to others. There will always be someone you think has more or has less of whatever you think will make you happy. Guess what? With gratitude, you can be happy right now!

Plus, when we are grateful, we are more likely to be happy for others. When you are happy, you naturally want the same for everyone else, which can be a powerful force for good.

Another benefit of gratitude is that it dissolves compulsive wanting. With just a little more gratitude in their attitude, shopaholics may even become minimalists! Think about it. It's a no-brainer that if we are satisfied with all we have, then we need less.

The answer is within. Actor Jim Carrey said, "I wish everyone could get rich and famous and have everything they ever dreamed of so they could see that it is not the answer." That is why meditation and affirmations help build our mental strength and our gratitude practice. Through meditation, we can change our thinking to "I am happy with what I already have. I have so much to be grateful for." True abundance begins with the thoughts we choose for ourselves.

The next time you are meditating with your eyes closed and in a relaxed state of mind, imagine that you have the life of a billionaire with every material wish you have ever dreamed of. Having everything you could possibly pay for, what would you value the most? It would be the same things you value now! People and experiences are the most priceless and valuable part of life and always will be. So, together, let's explore the richest parts of your fortunate existence.

Let's start with the priceless experience of strong, loving relationships. Bring to mind the people in your life that support you and thank them. Feel gratitude for the ones who were there in your past, the ones in your present, and the ones who will be there in your future, including both friends and family. Without an awkward real-life moment, you can use your imagination to thank them for the lessons they have taught you about yourself and for allowing you into their life. With your mind's eye and in your heart, make sure they know you appreciate them. When we are grateful for others, it opens the door to giving and receiving love unconditionally.

Remember that "as the mind conceives, the body must achieve" is one of the laws of the mind. "Imagination is more important than knowledge," said Einstein—a scientist! The body can't tell the difference between an image in the mind and what we call reality. Test this yourself by imagining you are biting into a lemon without salivating.

Extend gratitude to all parts of yourself, and yes, I do mean the outside too. The outer body is the part of us we are constantly criticizing. We are hardest on our physical body, always putting it down in some way. Imagine looking in the mirror one day and not wanting to change a thing instead of seeing only what you don't like. You could feel good about everything you see in that reflection, feeling good inside and out, exactly as you are.

Let's begin with our skin. Love the skin you're in by being present with it exactly as it is, strengthening the mind-body connection by listening to your intuition. Remember that skin is the largest organ of the body, and studies suggest that skin cells respond favorably to meditation and positive affirmations. Stop complaining about your various colors and markings, your state of moistness or dryness, the fine lines and wrinkles that make you uniquely wonderful. Loving your skin as it is while listening to your intuition will help it achieve a balanced state because you will take care of it lovingly—with a moisturizer or a trip to a dermatologist or just pure and simple acceptance.

Meditation comes to the rescue here too! It is a practical way for the entire self—mind, body, and spirit—to achieve health, skin care included. Meditation is good for you, but did you know how good it is for your skin? A little known side effect from meditation is an acceleration of the healing process in skin cells.

Many beginning meditators have noticed remarkable changes for the better in the quality of their facial skin. Relaxation of facial muscles naturally decreases wrinkles. Another regular occurrence is a noticeable rapid healing of blemishes and burns.

The body's ability to self-repair has been verified scientifically. In her comprehensively researched *Mind Over Medicine*, Dr. Lissa Rankin writes that "the body is a self-healing organism, constantly striving to return to homeostasis."

Applying a few mental training techniques while in a state of deep meditation will support that system and give it the right environment in which to work. Achieve a healthy glow from the inside out with visualization.

Introducing positive images while in this deeply relaxed state can be highly effective. Mind-body pioneers Bellaruth Naparstek and Shakti Gawain accept this simple, profound fact. They recommend deliberately adding healthful images to "the gullible body." Using your mind's eye, see the problem once, fix it, and then only see the positive outcome any time you think about it. By moving past the problem, you reinforce a positive result.

The very way the cells work in the body is magical. Eighty million white blood cells are produced inside you per minute as our first line of defense from a burn or injury. Focusing on these "soldier" cells can be effective on that cellular level.

Even showering skin cells in white light or mentally applying a "special" lotion will focus your repair response. Be creative. Mentally experience your new, fabulous self and skin in a multisensory way, engaging all five senses. Your imagination will come up with a visual remedy that suits you best. Try these affirmations too:

> I have smooth, soft, youthful, radiant skin.
> I have glowing, moist skin.
> My skin reflects my inner peace.
> I have clear, healthy skin.

You get the idea. For remarkable results on the outside, try a little work on the inside.

Next, scan your body with gratitude just like you do when you release stress and spread relaxation at the beginning of your meditation practice or in bed at the end of a hectic day.

Extending your focus from the few parts that aren't perfect to the 99 percent that actually are working at an optimal level can make you grateful for waking up another day. My dad has had a couple of heart attacks. When I ask him in the morning how he is, he always replies, "Another day cheating death is a good day."

The process of loving your body starts by giving thanks to it. The body is a self-healing organism, always striving to return us to a state of balance. Recognize the demands we place on this miraculous mechanism with gratitude.

Begin this gratitude process by slowly going through the outer parts of your body—fingers and toes and everything in between. Go into as much detail as possible by being grateful for your brain and moving down the body, thanking each organ, all the way to your feet that move you on command from one place to another on this planet. But don't forget the body's inner wonders. Feel gratitude for the internal organs that silently work behind the scenes of your consciousness to keep you alive.

When you say thank you with sincerity and compassion, your body will thank you back with good health, strength, and resiliency. Say thank you to your heart, thank you to your lungs, thank you to your digestion, thank you to your nervous system, thank you to every single cell. Thank you, thank you! You cannot say it too many times. Flood your amazing body with love and the light of thankfulness. As you become lighthearted and full of gratitude, you will move through this world with a grace that is noticeable and contagious.

Being grateful for your physical form in this way is an excellent method of shifting perception from disappointment and disgust to appreciation when you look in the mirror. This is vital on your journey to unconditional self-love. As often as possible, practice seeing your body for the miracle it is.

Now we know that an attitude of gratitude accelerates the healing processes of the body, put it into practice by promising to make healthy choices to support its work.

And don't forget to be grateful for all the people that come into our life. We can have the experience of meeting new people from around the world. A stranger is just a friend we haven't connected with yet. Be grateful to discover that we are all the same. We all have love and gratitude in our hearts just waiting to be released and recognized. See the similarities and be thankful for your part in this human experience.

Be grateful too for all the heartfelt experiences in the past and still to come that deliver joy and happiness. Think about the joy of a child's innocent smile and giggle.

Be thankful for all the wonderful feelings and emotions that come your way. Emotions are just energy in motion. Good or bad, be grateful to have all feelings as they come and go with ease, allowing you to connect to the ebb and flow of your life. On the positive side, a good belly laugh is priceless. Shedding tears of tenderness when your heart is touched by a meaningful photograph or story is a genuine experience not to be taken for granted.

Give thanks as well to the music that helps you express yourself. Dancing and singing to music can inspire and relax. Music can instantly change our vibration. Be thankful for the musicians and artists that share their expressive souls with us. We can harness the power of music for our journey to self-love. Hearing Whitney Houston sing "the greatest love of all is inside of me" gives me goosebumps!

Be grateful for all aspects of your life. A pet that licks your nose when you first wake up is a true joy. The purring and pushing of a cute loving cat is something special to be grateful for. Notice how our pets never turn their backs on us. They never give us the silent treatment. They embody unconditional love and forgiveness. These precious souls teach us how to love and accept ourselves as we are, no matter what kind of day we had.

Nature is another treasured part of life that is always available to us. Interacting with ocean beaches, flower gardens, trees in a forest, and mountain ranges will help us connect to that still, peaceful place within. It only takes a moment to stop and look up at the sun, or at clouds, blue sky, sunset colors, or the moon and stars, to become aware of the miracle of life that surrounds us. Appreciate the way Mother Earth provides us with nutrition, oxygen, and hydration to bring us back to balance on every level.

Take mindful moments to see and feel your connection to earthly wonders by breathing mindfully while walking barefoot to ground and connect to the biomagnetic field of the Earth. Earthing is a practice that uses the electrons from the Earth's surface to have a healthy, anti-inflammatory effect on our bodies. Realize you are a part of nature in order to experience an improvement in your well-being.

Our goal is to become grateful for all that is deep and soulful, for the inner wealth of valuable and precious experiences, and for the world around us. It remains up to us to become more aware and grateful with each new day.

Every day is a gift. Adding an element of appreciation will do wonders for you, no matter what your bank account is, or what you weigh, or your marital status, or your race or gender. It will help us look through any difficulties toward a positive direction no matter the outer circumstances. When you drop the victim mentality and add gratitude to your day, you allow happiness to bubble up to the surface where it belongs.

Showing gratitude means showing love. Seeing love and feeling love can be as simple as appreciating the smallest thing about yourself. Being grateful leads to extending love to all aspects of yourself. Where focus goes, energy flows; so let's focus on that and get positive energy flowing in your own deserving direction.

We have to thank ourselves for balancing our inner and outer lives with meditation, gratitude, and love, and to remember to pay it forward, turning the positive flow of energy from a trickle to a flood that can affect everyone in our lives and everyone on the planet.

PRACTICE

Begin an appreciation journal. Keep it next to your bed, and before going to sleep, add at least one new person, place, or experience that you are grateful for. Doing the same when you wake up will set you up for a happy day.

Seventeenth-century philosopher Baruch Spinoza suggested asking yourself three questions:

> Who or what inspired me today?
> What brought me happiness today?
> What brought me comfort and deep peace today?

Performing this practice daily will reinforce looking for the positive things that lead to a greater appreciation for life.

15

UNIVERSAL LOVE

Radiate boundless love toward the entire world.
—BUDDHA

Yes, it is time to take your love of self out into the world. Just like in the airplane when we place the oxygen mask on ourselves so we can then help the child next to us, as your own internal well of love overflows, you will have the resources to be of greater service to others.

Be careful, as your confusion over why you are here, what your purpose is, and finding your passion can also show up as self-pressure and a mind trick to trap you into judging yourself too harshly for not doing enough for the world. It can trigger the perfectionist. Just notice it, smile, move forward with a little note to self: "It's OK when I notice the demands I place on myself. I am perfectly imperfect." You can avoid the trap of "should-ing" yourself with unrealistic expectations by lightening up and focusing your talents in effective ways—locally and within your network, slowly yet intentionally. You will find that your network will expand and more positive people and events will come to your aid. Your transition into a loving being that radiates love will happen through service to others.

Releasing the need to criticize and compare yourself to others not only allows more peace into your life but contributes to world peace by rippling out the vibration of peace and love. This ripple effect is real, according to quantum physics and the superstring theory: everything is connected, and there is no time or distance between thoughts and energy.

You can't be there for others when you are depleted and so down on yourself that you create more stress in everyone's life. The people who depend on you need you to be healthy and happy. You are doing everyone a favor by showing up for yourself, by prioritizing self-care and investing in your mental, physical, and spiritual health. We need more than a cup of self-love for our immediate connections and for the planet. We are worthy of an entire ocean of love so it can flood out to the universe. Loving yourself fully and effectively is what you need so you can continue to contribute to the greater good of all.

You can unlock your truth and share from this growing reservoir of self-love by looking for ways to serve. The goodness you bring to your community will in turn feed into the self-worth, and voila, you have replaced the cycle of loathing with a cycle of loving.

Your talents are now out of the box and able to shine brightly. Brightly enough to illuminate the path for others. Your service begins where you are right now. It does not need to be grandiose or an expensive enterprise. A simple act of kindness, like a smile or giving an unexpected compliment, can brighten someone's day and give them greatly needed faith in humanity or lift a mood or inspire another act of kindness as they pay it forward. You never know the chain reaction of love you can create right now where you live!

I am a very positive person (in case you didn't notice), and it is so funny to see the reaction I get from people who are exposed to a positive viewpoint about something that they could only see as gloomy and depressing. For example, a friend was lamenting his tragic predicament of having to move unexpectedly, holding onto contempt for his landlady. I listened, and I reminded him that he wanted a bigger place with less rent and to be near a park, so wasn't this great that he was free to move to a better place? How wonderful for him; how lucky and blessed he was. The look of shock on his face as he realized that was a truth he'd only just considered was priceless. Spreading peace through the world could mean offering a best-case scenario to someone rather that wallowing in pity. He was now able to be grateful to his landlady, and that thought alone was a relief to all involved. It's as if you lit a candle in a dark room or cracked open a door to let in a sliver of light. My attitude is that who knows where that ray of optimism and hope might lead?

The outside world is a reflection of our inner world. But how can we impact the world in a positive way if we are projecting the harsh judgments we hold for ourselves? We need, first, to actualize our truth, which is love, to then make a meaningful contribution not just for our close relationships but for all beings.

The human race is not done with evolution. We are embarking on the next stage of it—and no, I do not mean that babies will be born with smaller thumbs for texting! I refer to the collective consciousness of all sentient beings on our planetary maternal Earth. When we evolve, the world gets a little closer to the title of Malcom Gladwell's book *The Tipping Point*. This refers to the critical mass needed for ideas and behaviors to spread in the manner viruses do.

Think of how contagious yawning is. Even reading the word and imagining a yawn can create the physical response of opening your mouth wide and—yawning. I use this example at the beginning of all my Befriend Your Sleep classes or sleep meditations. It really is a remarkable way, even on Zoom with a global audience, to shift consciousness from a wakeful state to prepare to shut down and morph into sleep mode together as a group.

According to social scientists, everything has a tipping point, a critical mass, a threshold, a boiling point, or a breaking point. As personal compassion spreads around the world, people will begin to break through the negative bias and fear-based judgments they have grown too comfortable living with. Musicians and peace activists John Lennon and Yoko Ono gifted us with the visionary anthem "Imagine," making just this point. As we approach and surpass the tipping point, the unexpected will become expected, rendering radical change more than a possibility. It will become a certainty.

We hold the key to turn our metaphorical boat around before it goes over the waterfall. We have the power of our attention. Where focus goes, energy flows. (That can never be said enough times!)

Politics can still be invested in without losing your head over it. Just take back some control. There was a guy I liked that wouldn't date me because I didn't watch CNN all the time, so I could not give him my detailed opinion of Ron DeSantis. Sheesh! Get a life. A life that dwells on positive impact rather than feeling helpless and hopeless while glued to a screen controlled by mass media conglomerates. You can be a part of something bigger and be the change through direct involvement, such as volunteering.

I should say that my political life is important to me, and I believe voting is a form of love in action, but I would rather place my focus on creating positive content and teaching peace. The world needs positivity in any form to balance out the constant churning of suffering, stress, and doomsday predictions.

Let's start to contribute to some best-case scenario predictions. Placing pebbles of peace into the pond of pure potentiality is more important than the latest scandal. There is power in the number of these pebbles!

Believe it or not, studies confirm that when a group meditates together, there is a ripple effect of peace in the surrounding environment. According to superstring theory, vibrational waves flow from everything in the universe, affecting the collective consciousness of others. Groups can enliven that field. In *The Biology of Belief: Unleashing the Power of Consciousness, Matter & Miracles*, cellular biologist Bruce Lipton says the universe is made of energy and that our consciousness can change the physical world around us by altering the quantum field with our own energetic awareness as thoughts are energy too.

Japanese scientist, Dr. Masaru Emoto has studied the effect of human consciousness on water, finding that emotional energies and vibrations can change its physical structure. His experiments exposed glasses of water to different words, pictures, or music. He then froze the water to examine the formation of crystals under a microscope. The conclusion revealed that water exposed to positive speech and thoughts results in visually appealing crystal structures. In contrast, water exposed to negative words and thoughts results in asymmetrical, disturbing, and incomplete crystal patterns. You can see these wonders on YouTube at "Water, Consciousness & Intent: Dr. Masaru Emoto."

It will give you something to think about since most of the human body is water, roughly 60 percent. I wonder what my water crystals look like, don't you? I want beautiful patterns in my body, and that keeps me speaking to myself with kindness.

Another experiment testing the superstring theory was undertaken over three years in Merseyside, England. A small percentage of the population (just over one percent) meditated together every day from 1988 to1991, Merseyside's crime rate dropped so much that it went from third highest to the lowest ranked city in the UK during the time of the analysis. Meanwhile, another neighborhood was used as the control town of non-meditators, which held a steady crime rate. Meditation was the only factor in the study that could account for the change. (Police practices, local economics, and demographics remained the same throughout the study.) This was called the Maharishi Effect because the community practiced Transcendental Meditation (TM) as taught by the Maharishi International University.

I believe that a mass awakening to love has already begun, and just like the controversial hundredth monkey effect, we may reach a critical number where the world literally wakes up or opens up some new neural pathways of compassionate perception.

This "effect" is from a study in which Japanese primatology scientists recorded the behavior of a troop of macaque monkeys on Kashima Island for over thirty years. Of note, they provided the monkeys with sweet potatoes, and one day a young macaque they had named Imo walked to the ocean to wash off the dirt and sand before eating her potato.

What caused this sudden change? I have a theory based on studies that show that *how* you look at things actually *changes* what you are looking at.

According to the observer effect, subatomic particles appear to exist only as a wave of probabilities *until* being observed, at which time they collapse into a single place in time. This suggests that there is no reality until that reality is perceived. This profound insight tells us that we alter every object in the world simply by paying attention to it. If you are unhappy with a certain experience, you can choose to steer your focus toward something else that is aligned with your own positive expectations.

I have a theory—as far as I know, I am the only one to come up with it—and because this is my book, I am going to go ahead and put it out there. I believe that it truly bothered the Japanese researchers who had to endure watching the primates eat dirt along with the vegetable. Accuse me of stereotyping if you must, but Japanese culture is a beautiful society of scrupulously beheld cleanliness. I think that from their observation point, those scientists were unawarely mentally willing and visualizing—almost begging—the monkeys to wash their potatoes. It was bugging them!

I further believe that Imo, the young macaque, had an open alpha state connected to the universal mind. She resonated with the scientists visions of their preferred behavior and acted on it. She then taught other youngsters who taught the elders in the troop. This in itself was groundbreaking because in nature it is almost always the older parental figures that model behavior for the babies, handing information *down*. Imo, however, handed the information *around*, and the youngsters cumulatively handed it *up*!

Skeptic Boyce Rensberger came up with the "Spud-Dunking Monkey Theory." He said that the washing of the sandy sweet potatoes increased at a normal rate, with some older monkeys still eating the dirty ones five years later.

Then something startling took place. (Here I am indebted to Ken Keyes Jr.'s book *The Hundredth Monkey*.)

No one really knows the exact number, but one hundred is just an easy way to describe it. Let us suppose that when the sun rose one morning, there were ninety-nine monkeys on Kashima Island that had learned to wash their sweet potatoes, and then a new hundredth monkey learned to wash potatoes.

According to Keyes, by that evening every member of the troop was washing before eating. Then scientists on the other islands observed that this new habit spontaneously jumped over the sea. Colonies of monkeys separated by water, on other islands, and the mainland troop at Takasakiyama began washing their sweet potatoes!

This is an established scientific experiment that demonstrates when a certain critical number of macaques (I am adding the assumption of humans too) achieves an awareness, this new awareness can be communicated mind to mind within the species. In Imo's case, the added energy of the hundredth monkey somehow created a radical breakthrough. This strongly suggests that only one more person (or monkey) tuning in to a new awareness can sufficiently strengthen a field to facilitate the transmission of that awareness to the greater tribe. Rupert Sheldrake cited that this phenomenon would be evidence of morphic fields effecting consciousness and learning.

Your awareness is needed in saving the world! Who knows, you may be the hundredth monkey in your group. You may furnish the added consciousness so urgently needed to create a compassionate society with loving values.

The above concept is confirmed, according to Ken Keyes Jr., Lyall Watson, Carl Rogers, and other scientists and theorists. Watson states it as "The appreciation and love we have for ourselves and others creates an expanding energy field that becomes a growing power in the world."

Two salient quotes come to mind. First, as Margaret Mead said, "Never doubt that a small group of people can change the world. Indeed it is the only thing that ever has." Second, the great Marianne Williamson, in her groundbreaking *A Return to Love*, says that "our deepest fear is that we are powerful beyond measure. It is our light, not our darkness, that most frightens us." Williamson makes clear that we need a mass awakening.

The time has come to use your power to shift the tides of self-hate to love for all. Imagine people all over the world dropping their weapons, waking up from a foggy sleep, wondering how they could have ever hurt anyone else, and only seeing the light in the other's eyes. In fact, as we become one human family, there are no "others" to hate anymore. No egos or fear so no need to divide; and the only thing to conquer is the resistance to love for all of humanity. A namaste world where all are honored for their shared humanitarian values and communitarian concerns. There is plenty of everything for everyone.

Self-love runs deep. Deeper than the outer identities that separate us from each other. Deeper than gender, occupation, political party, bank account, age, race, where we come from, and how we look. Self-love removes the barriers to oneness; it allows us to see our deep connection as one humanity with all our brothers and sisters sharing this planet. According to *The Course in Miracles*, there is only one of us here, and therefore, when we love ourselves, we are loving all.

Self-love becomes love in action. Taking our me-love and sharing it as we-love. Happiness and peace are contagious, and we almost can't help but spread it around. You are now available to be of service at a deeper level and wider capacity than ever before. You will find it so much easier and natural to contribute to society and serve all beings by being love in action.

Spread love by being love. You have something authentic and valuable to share with others to make a contribution to the world. This altruism creates a joyous cycle of giving and receiving that compounds and expands happiness the world over.

So get busy living a life of love!

PRACTICE

Draw a heart on a page with your name in it. Write your circles of connection on the page around it. Friends, family, work, and acquaintances. It will show you how many you can have an impact on with your one precious life, and how often. It doesn't have to be on the world stage, although it could lead anywhere you want it to.

If you feel limited, lonely, or depressed, try volunteering at a place that you have an affinity toward. By helping others, you help yourself. You can also find an internship to make friends and feel productive and purposeful. (I volunteered for Marianne Williamson's presidential campaign and sold T-shirts at her Oakland event. I shook hands with her and was able to look into her eyes and tell her she was doing a great job. It was very rewarding.)

Thank you for following me on this journey to true love for our true selves. This is a lifelong process, and luckily it is never too late to begin. Most importantly, thank yourself for taking this quality time for your self-care. Remember who your best friend is. Befriend yourself with all the love you deserve. Lighten up! You are worthy of love because you are love and light.

ABOUT THE AUTHOR

Kathryn Remati writes and records guided meditations for everyone to access inner peace. She is a true master at leading even the most stressed to their center of calm. She has meditated since age sixteen, and is a certified meditation instructor with a BA in psychology and a masters from the University of New South Wales in Sydney, where she grew up. Presently, traveling the world as a digital nomad minimalist, she worked as a Kaiser Permanente Health Educator, teaching classes for insomnia, weight, and stress management. *USA Today* and *Health Daily* have both listed her as one of the top ten meditation teachers to follow in 2022.

When a fire-walking, ice bathing, chanting, yoga enthusiast, plant medicine warrior, and meditation teacher develops an app for inner peace, you know it will be unique. And her popular *Tranquil Me* meditation app is all that and more. After meditating for forty years, she says "If someone had predicted back in college that I could reach so many at once through their phones, it would have been hard to imagine it as anything but science fiction." Luckily, due to the miracle of technology, we can have peace right in our pocket. Kathryn is now devoting her life to spreading inner peace, and she over-delivers with a side of love, fun, and happiness. Peace is now possible anywhere, anytime, for anyone.

After Kathryn had trouble finding everything she likes from different platforms, she made sure the *Tranquil Me* meditation app is compatible with both iPhones and Androids and works on airplane mode without Wi-Fi or paying extra. (She used to have to use four different types of apps when traveling from Sydney to Boston.)

She says, "I created all the meditations to include binaural beats to rapidly lower brainwaves, and with affirmations for reprogramming." The app has nature sounds for visualizing and tricking your mind to receive the benefits of being in nature. You can also toggle the sound mix for voice and music that is perfect for you, or only for background music if that is all you need at that time.

A good meditation app is the easiest way to reset and balance our body and mind for a happy and healthy life. "I figured if I built one I liked," she says, "others would also like it, and it will help relieve the high levels of anxiety becoming a part of our society of stress. You can experience peace in your daily life, thereby contributing to world peace, one peaceful person at a time and 'be the change' we need in this world."

Peace may be her mission, but her heart longed for motherhood and she was truly blessed with two amazing human beings that despite her limited role models and huge learning curve as a parent, her children managed to achieve incredible success in their lives. She is the proud parent of a Cancer scientist and an Olympic level athlete. These two will always be her most precious contribution to the world. They make her life more meaningful and fill her heart with joy no matter where life leads her.

ACKNOWLEDGMENTS

I would like to thank my publishers for their patience as life kept me meandering through more and more lessons to learn. When I finally had a complete manuscript, what a blessing to have the assistance of enthusiastic and talented editor extraordinaire, Kurt Lipschutz. Thank you, Kurt, for your daunting dedication to excellence.

Huffpost, OmTimes, Yoga International, and other magazines published my early articles about meditation. Though I am a first-time book author, their support gave me the confidence and audacity to eventually create *Befriend Yourself.*

Decades of reading inspirational writers went into these pages. Those voices tapped into the universal mind and brought their message to light up the world, and in so doing lit up my world.

During a four-day retreat in the Blue Mountains, author and teacher Stuart Wilde taught me to face my fears and rise. He awarded me a Popeye fridge magnet with the words "I am what I am." He also demonstrated that in order to help others, it is not necessary to be a perfect enlightened being living a perfectly healthy life. Further, he taught me to just be myself and have fun—and not to take life too seriously. He is on the other side of the veil with Dr. Wayne Dyer, who inspired me to not give up, and reminded me that life is short so I had best get to work to leave behind something of value.

The work of Marianne Williamson was the inspiration for the last chapter. Her lectures on A Course in Miracles and her heartfelt writing guided me through many relationships and personal struggles. She sets the example of being a channel for creativity, love, and change, which the world so needs.

Thank you also to Oprah Winfrey for giving inspirational, spiritual, personal-growth writers an international platform. Through her love of books, Oprah pioneered and normalized opening one's heart and mind to alternate, deeply personal, therapeutic perspectives accessible to all. I was once one of the millions of housewives that waited all day for her show to come on to add some inspiration to my day full of diapers and dirty little feet.

This undertaking would not have been possible without the love and support from my sisterhood of friendships spanning the globe. These special women always saw the best in me even when I could not. You know who you are.

Thank you to Robert R Abbott AKA Bud who believed in my abilities enough to finance our first few Lighten Up retreats and show me the beauty of Costa Rica where I wrote one of my favorite chapters to this book.

And how could I write a self-love guide without acknowledging my lifelong commitment to personal growth? I knew I had a book in me but had to peel back many layers to find it. It could not have been born without my optimism and ability to bounce back. I am grateful for my often painful, unrelenting excavation through my many roles and identities and the rubble of my past, as I built a brighter, lighter future with bricks of love.

Most importantly, I thank my talented and precious children. These two wise, old souls continue to teach me the true meaning of unconditional love and forgiveness. Without them, I might not be alive today. I hope to be like them when I grow up.

Disclaimer: The information provided is subjective and based on personal research and results and is not intended to be a substitute for professional medical advice, diagnosis, or treatment. Please refer all mental health concerns to your qualified healthcare provider.

Printed in Great Britain
by Amazon